You are Loved

Anna D'Amato

Angels Share the Power of
"I Love Me"

How It Can Change Your
Life and the World

Aura D'Amato

BALBOA.
PRESS

A DIVISION OF HAY HOUSE

Aura D'Amato's, Website: angelsguidedhealing.com

Eva M. Sakmar-Sullivan, Website: stardolphin.com

Balboa Press books may be ordered through booksellers or by contacting:

Balboa Press
A Division of Hay House
1663 Liberty Drive
Bloomington, IN 47403
www.balboapress.com
1 (877) 407-4847

Print information available on the last page.

ISBN: 978-1-5043-2563-9 (sc)
ISBN: 978-1-5043-2565-3 (hc)
ISBN: 978-1-5043-2564-6 (e)

Library of Congress Control Number: 2014922401

Balboa Press rev. date: 03/13/2015

Contents

You Walk Your Path In The Company Of Angels

Angels are always with you and accompany you on each step that you take. They communicate with you and assist you in many ways. They provide insight and guidance on your path. They remind you that you were chosen to shine God's light and to share His love on your journey, and they assist you in doing so. Angels flash thoughts of wisdom and inspiration through your mind, and inspire others to bring you messages of love. They bring you a sense of peace during challenging times, and remove obstacles that hinder your way. Angels come to assure you of how profoundly loved you are and the magnitude of God's power that is within you.

Ask your angels to converse with you and they will do so. There are many ways that angels communicate with you. They may give you awareness or insight on which direction to take. They may come to you through a vision or bring a message to you through the spoken word of another. Angels are your ever present and loving companions who seek God's will in being of service to you. You need only to ask for their intervention and they will joyfully be of assistance to you. The choice is yours to accept the love of your angels and the gift of God's love within you.

The symbol below was given to me by the angels. It is a Divinely empowered symbol infused with Divine love, light and energy. It is intended to empower those who view it or have it in their presence with God's love, light and energy. The angels guided me to put this symbol in this book to convey that these angelic messages are Divinely inspired, and that God's love, light and energy are being sent forth.

Acknowledgements

I give all glory and praise to God, Jesus Christ, the Holy Spirit, and the Archangels Michael, Jophiel, Chamuel, Gabriel, Raphael, Uriel, Zadkiel and their team of angels for the Divine messages that are shared in this book. I acknowledge all praise and honor to them for the Divine love, light, energy, power, inspiration, enlightenment, guidance and healing that goes forth as a result of these angelic messages. With a thankful heart, I humbly accept my role as an angel communicator to share this angelic message of the power of proclaiming *"I love me,"* and how it can profoundly change our lives and the world. I acknowledge with gratitude the presence of God and His angels who are always with us and who bring forth love into our lives.

I give my heartfelt thanks to my family whose love, support and guidance helped make it possible for the angelic messages in this book to be published. I am profoundly grateful to God for my loving family and for my angel companions who are always with me guiding my way.

The "Angel Of Love" Painting

The painting on the cover of this book is called "Angel Of Love." It was Divinely inspired by the angels. It became a work of art through the artistic talent of its painter, Eva M. Sakmar-Sullivan. It was through Divine and angel intervention that Eva and I met. I had asked the angels for guidance on which angel picture to use for the cover of this book. One day, while scrolling through angel pictures on the computer, an angel painted by Eva popped up on my screen along with a link to her website. After reading about Eva on her website, viewing her gallery of pictures, and asking for Divine guidance, I felt assured that Eva had been chosen to paint the "Angel Of Love" painting. I contacted Eva and shared with her that I was publishing a book of angel messages that had been Divinely given to me. I told Eva I was given angelic guidance that described what the angel picture on the cover of the book was to look like. Eva enthusiastically agreed to be a part of this Divine process. It was then that I commissioned her to paint the "Angel Of Love" painting.

Eva's Comments About "The Angel Of Love" Painting

"This painting was a work of love between the angels, Aura and myself. I am deeply honored to have been chosen to paint the 'Angel Of Love' and I gladly accepted the direction that the angels gave me through Aura's vision.

Inspiration for the painting came in many ways. I relied on prayer, meditation and trust. When I picked a canvas for the painting, the angels seemed to say, I would need more room, so I chose a larger canvas. With the added space of the new, larger canvas, something miraculous happened. The rays of love that sweep up from the angel's heart to the Divine symbol above the crown of the angel formed a heart! The heart was never planned, but appeared as I finished the painting. The heart symbolizes what the painting is about - Divine Love.

The sparkles and starbursts in the painting are symbolic of the many legions of angels that are with us to meet all of our needs. The circles with symbols are called Light Language. They were painted with the highest intention to bring forth Divine love, healing, clarity, wisdom and peace. Their purpose is to help awaken these Divine intentions within the heart of the viewer. I mixed three types of Quartz Crystal into the paint- Amethyst, Rose Quartz and Clear Quartz to bring forth the highest vibration of Divine love.

The symbol within the angel's heart was specifically designed with guidance from the angels. This symbol holds blessings and frequencies as they were given by the angels to Aura to send forth Divine love, light, energy, wisdom, peace, joy and inspiration to those who view the painting."

May blessings go forth to all,

Eva M. Sakmar-Sullivan

What The Angels Revealed About "The Angel Of Love" Painting

The "Angel Of Love" painting came about through Divine guidance, inspiration and intervention. While writing this book, I received an angelic message that the angel picture on the cover of this book would have a profound loving and powerful affect upon those who viewed it and upon the world. I was given specific directions on what the angel picture should entail and that it was to be called Angel Of Love. Above the crown of the angel's head is the symbol of the Divinity of God The Father, The Son, and The Holy Spirit. Flowing through this symbol is the vibrant white light of God that bursts forth in colorful rays of light. These colorful rays of light flow through the angel's heart, and back to the symbol of the Divinity of God, forming a heart shape. The formation of the heart in this painting was not planned nor did the painter design it with intention. The heart took on form upon the completion of the painting through Divine intervention. The heart shape symbolizes the angelic message of Divine love and how each of us is Divinely connected to God's love and light. The rays of different colors of light within the painting represent the vibrant white light of God and the colors of the seven Archangels Michael, Jophiel, Chamuel, Gabriel, Raphael, Uriel, and Zadkiel. There are symbols in the painting and within the angel's heart that were inspired by the angels to hold Divine energetic frequencies, love, light and blessings. It is the intention through these symbols to send forth Divine love, light, energy, wisdom, peace, joy, inspiration and blessings to those who view the painting. The angel's face in this painting represents features and characteristics of people from all walks of life. The message being shared through this painting is that each of us is created from God's love, and we have the power of God's love, and the companionship of angels with us always. The Angel Of Love painting symbolizes our heart connection to the Divine love of God, and our companionship with His loving and powerful angels.

When you view this painting, see yourself surrounded by the love of God and His ministering angels. Allow God's vibrant white light to flow from the crown of your head through your heart and back to the symbol of the Divinity of God at your crown. Repeat these words *"I love me."* This is symbolic of

God's Divine love that flows from God within each of us bringing forth God's power and love.

May love go forth through "The Angel Of Love" painting and through these angelic messages to bring God's love and healing to you and to the world.

May God's love and light go forth to all,
Aura D'Amato

Prints of the "Angel Of Love" painting are available at angelsguidedhealing.com

An Angel Message Of Reflection

My Dearest Children,

It is with love that we converse with you this day. It gives us exuberant joy to be the bearers of God's messages of love for you. We come to share the truth of how truly loved you are and the importance of your place in God's creation of the world. Your life has supreme meaning, and all that you are designed to be has supreme meaning.

You have the light of God within you, which is connected to all that is of God. You are the light that was sent forth as the vessel of God's love in human form. By choosing to say *"I love me,"* you are saying, "I love God who is within me." In proclaiming *"I love me,"* God's light within you expands out into your world and brings forth joyful and empowering living.

There is an abundance of God's light and love within you. You are created to shine forth the light of God for the glory of His love to be known. God's light holds the supreme power, wisdom, truth, and love of your Creator. You have been given God's exuberant light, which contains all that is required for you to be an expression of God's love. There is no power greater than the love of God within you. You have the authority to call forth God's light and love to manifest the magnificence of who God is within you.

We, your angels, come to assist and accompany you on your journey in God's light. We come to share with you the meaning of *"I love me,"* and how it can bring the power of God's light and love to your experiences. Your life was designed and created from God's love. You are infinitely connected to all that God is. As you say *"I love me,"* and choose to send forth God's light, love will radiate through you and manifest miraculous expressions of God's existence. You shall call forth God's power for healing of body, mind, and spirit, and God's power shall go forth.

We joyfully share with you the powerful meaning of the expression *"I love me,"* and how these words can create changes of great magnitude to alter the face of the world. All is possible when you choose to love and honor God by saying *"I love me."* God's infinite power and love are being revealed each moment in you. As your angel companions and guides, God has given us the power to assist you in this awareness and to intervene in all areas of your life. We have the authority to bring forth God's rays of light for your healing and well-being. As you make your requests known, we will joyfully assist you. We assure you, as you say *"I love me,"* and honor the creation of God within you, you will experience the loving and powerful presence of God in your life's journey.

God designed for you to be in a joyful knowing of who you are. We come to remove the veil of unknowing and to awaken you to this glorious state of being. When God breathed life into you, it brought forth the magnificence of God's Divinity with all wisdom and truth, for you to become a reflection of His essence. Your life has supreme importance in the kingdom of God. You are designed to shine forth God's light within you for the glory of God to be made known.

God's essence of unwavering love and Divine power is within you. You have a connection through God's essence that unites you with all creation and from which God's power flows. In this time of spiritual renewal and rejoicing, you are being guided to accept God's essence and unwavering love. You do this in the acknowledgment of the love of yourself and through the proclamation of *"I love me."*

"I love me" is a Divinely empowered phrase that brings forth your soul's connection to the joy, love, and omnipresent power of God. It is your choice to

say *"I love me,"* and to rise up in joyful adoration for God's presence within you. When these three powerful words are spoken you become a vessel from which God's love and power flow. Speak these words *"I love me,"* and you shall manifest God's presence to the farthest ends of the earth and beyond.

All that we do is for the glory of God. When we share God's messages and healing rays of light, we do so to give honor and praise to God. By choosing to say *"I love me,"* you, too, give honor and praise to God. In proclaiming *"I love me,"* you accept the love of God within you and it then goes forth to create joyful and empowering living for you.

It is with exuberant love that we come to be with you on your golden journey in the light. We are forever by your side and our love for you is ever present. We are God's messengers who bring forth God's rays of light for your well-being and for the glory of God. We are sharing the messages in this book for you to know and understand the loving and powerful presence of God that is within you. We have brought this message of self-love to awaken you to the importance of loving yourself, and thus God who is within you. We invite you to begin in this moment by saying *"I love me."* When you do so, you shall honor God's creation of you and become the expression of God's love and presence in your world.

As you go forth and proclaim *"I love me,"* we will assist you in knowing and expressing the magnificence of God's love that is within you.

~Your Loving Angel Companions

Introduction

By Aura D'Amato

The angelic messages in this book reveal the powerful meaning of the words *"I love me"* and how they can bring forth victorious and joyful living into your life and into the world. Angels are with you in every moment and have God's authority to assist you in all areas of your life. They bring God's power to uplift your spirit and heal your body. They inspire you with God's wisdom and light the path before you. Angels do mighty works and assist you in the way that you need, for God is their source of power and love. They come to be your companions and to guide you, yet they always respect your free will as given by God.

The angelic messages in this book were revealed to me through my loving dialogue with angels. I am an angel communicator and I have had a loving dialogue and connection with angels for many years. I communicate angelic messages of love for God's love and power to go forth in the world. I have received countless angelic messages and I have witnessed the power of God's love that has created healing and abundance in my life and in the lives of people from all walks of life.

As you read this inspirational book you will learn from the angels the power that comes from saying *"I love me,"* and how truly loved and magnificent you are. This book will help you to understand the power of God's love that is within you to realize your dreams for an abundant, prosperous, peaceful and joyful way of living. These angelic messages are being given to assure you that God's love and essence are within you. When you say these three words *"I love me"* you acknowledge the presence of God's love within you, and you become one with God's essence to experience all that God has created for you. In loving yourself, God's love shall go forth to bring love and healing to all facets of your life and within the world. These messages are being shared for you to know and accept the joy of being the infinitely loved and powerful being that you truly are in your oneness with God.

Welcome to your journey of knowing the power that comes from saying *"I love me."* It shall help you to resonate God's abundant love, light and power that reside within you to become the infinitely loved and magnificent person you are created to be.

CHAPTER ONE

The Words "I Love Me" Can Change Your Life

The angelic message of the power of *"I love me"* is being shared so that you may know you are a creation of Divine love and light, and God's love resides within you. As we begin this journey to your understanding of the power of *"I love me,"* be assured that your angel companions are present with you to guide and assist you. They bring love, joy, enlightenment, peace and laughter into your experience. Angels joyfully illuminate the power of God's love and light within you. They remind you of the importance of who you are as a child of God.

Angels are with you in this moment. When you say *"I love me,"* you are surrounded by God's light, and angels join with you to bring forth God's love into all areas of your life. As you accept the love and light of God, changes of great magnitude can occur in your life. Within your soul is a connection to God's essence of unwavering love and power. By saying *"I love me,"* you align with God's unwavering love and power that can bring forth Divine wisdom, inspiration, abundance and healing. Divine truths are revealed to you of the power of God's light and love in your life when you choose to love, and when you say *"I love me."* As God's love overflows from within you, it goes out into your world with the power to create joyful and empowering living. God's love and light can overcome and dispel all negative forces and lower energies that create fear, anxiety, worry, doubt, judgment, hatred, and anger. Choosing to love yourself is choosing to be in God's dwelling place. In the dwelling place of God, there is God's unwavering love that creates joy, peace, harmony, and healing of all magnitudes.

God is a loving God and He created you with love. The presence of angels in your life is confirmation of God's love for you. You are the magnificent creation and expression of God's essence and unconditional love. Angels come to remind you of this. They are given the authority by God to love, inspire and protect you. They bring to your awareness the power and love of God's presence, grace, and supreme wisdom. As you dwell upon and recite *"I love me,"* God's power magnifies within you and flows out into your world. When you voice the words *"I love me,"* you are choosing to receive and bring forth uplifting and healing changes in your life and in the world.

When you say the words *"I love me,"* you are accepting God's love for you. As you accept God's love for you, you are accepting Divine intervention in your life. You may have a grand experience, or it may be a subtle one. You may have a peaceful calm come over you, receive an inspiration or answer to a prayer, enjoy harmony in your relationships, experience improved finances, get a job or a promotion, receive healing in mind, body, or spirit, or experience the intervention of an angel. Experiences may occur that bring you abundance and joy. People may come into your life to assist you and uplift you. Situations may manifest at the right time for your well-being with no explanation, except that it comes as a Divine intervention. All is possible through the love and power of God, and there are unlimited possibilities of what can Divinely occur.

Angels come to enlighten you to the truth of who God is and the immeasurable importance of who you are in God's eyes. This angelic message of the love and power that comes from saying *"I love me"* may profoundly change your life and the world. Celebrate with joy and rejoice, for as you proclaim the words *"I love me,"* you proclaim your acceptance of your Divine connection to God's light, love, and power. It is through your Divine connection to God that you can send forth love to bring harmony, healing and peace into your life and into the world.

This message of love is being shared so that you can experience these gifts of God within you:

- God's Presence
- God's Power
- God's Love
- God's Joy
- God's Wisdom
- God's Healing
- God's Truths
- God's Goodness
- God's Abundance
- God's Well-Being
- God's Light
- God's Magnificence Reflected in You

An Angel Message Of Refection

My Dearest Children,

We are here to align with God's light within you. You have been chosen to know this angelic message of the importance of proclaiming *"I love me,"* and to walk as we do within God's loving presence. We come to awaken you to all that has been given unto you for the expression of God's love and power.

You are like a flower in its seed form that is being magnified into the expression of beauty as you bloom forth. We are here to assist you to bloom forth into the expression of God's magnificence and love. This expression is in the seed of God's essence within you. You can water this seed with love by saying *"I love me."* As you do this, God's magnificent expression and power of who you are created to be shall bloom forth.

We come to line your path with our vibrant light to assure you that wherever you walk, we are there with you. It is a glorious day in God's light, for we come to celebrate with joy, God's creation of you.

~Your Loving Angel Companions

How *"I Love Me"* Empowers You

"I love me" is a proclamation of your love for the Divine presence of God that is in the creation of you. Loving you loves God who created you. By choosing to say *"I love me,"* you align with and become the expression of God's love and power that is within you. When you honor and praise God through the proclamation of *"I love me,"* your eyes will see, your heart will know, and your mind will understand the magnificence of who you are and the power of God within you to create a joyous, prosperous, and love-filled life.

You have an important role in the creation and flow of the universe. The gifts and treasures of God's wisdom and love that have been given unto you have an important purpose in life. God breathed life into you because He has a grand design for your life that only you can fulfill. Your life is of extreme importance in the kingdom of God. What God chose to bring forth in the creation of you has immeasurable value and purpose. You have all that is needed to be the expression of God's love and power. By saying *"I love me,"* you give your acceptance to receive the power of God's overflowing love and wisdom. You call forth the love and power of God that is within you to become God's expression of Divine love in human form. You have God's authority to share His healing power and love. When you join with others who choose to resonate God's love, you uplift the consciousness of your world to a loving state of being that will be reflected in your life experiences.

Angels heighten your awareness of God's love that is within you and assist you on your journey to experience God's love. It is the connection through God's love that joins all people in oneness with God and with each other. Angels are ever present in your life to enlighten you of the power you have to be a minister of love, peace and harmony in the world. All that is within you is a gift of God's love. When you honor the gift of you by saying *"I love me,"* you bring glory to God and blessings to yourself and others. *"I love me"* empowers you to be God's expression of love and power in your life.

What Love Is

Love is the highest vibration of energy that exists. All that is within the universe has a knowing of the supreme power of God's love.

It is from love that all in creation were formed and came into being.

It is from love that healing occurs.

It is from love that hearts are changed and bondages are broken.

It is from love that the supreme being of God resonates the essence of who you are.

It is from love that you experience joy.

It is from love that peace occurs.

It is love that brings forth God's light for the release of all negative thoughts, spirits and forces.

It is from love that you manifest God's power in your life.

In your choosing to love yourself, you are making it known to the universe that you are worthy of love, and that you are love.

Love is the most powerful force in the universe. There is nothing greater than the power of God's love. When you choose to say *"I love me,"* you are choosing to be in oneness with God. In your oneness with God, you have the power of God's love to forgive, to bring forth healing for yourself and others, and to affect the world.

You have a connection with God's love and power now in this moment. When you say *"I love me,"* you are opening the flow of God's love and Divine energy that connects all His creations together. Love is God's form of communication with you. It is how God speaks through your soul to awaken you to His love and wisdom, and all of the gifts He has created for you. When you say *"I love me,"* you are communicating with God.

The Power Of *"I Love Me"*

The proclamation *"I love me"* is your acceptance of God's love and power that is within you.

Proclaiming *"I love me"* Can Bring Forth:

- The unwavering love and power of God
- God's illuminating light
- God's exuberant joy and happiness
- Divine and angelic intervention
- The treasures of God's kingdom
- Abundant and prosperous living
- God's wisdom and truth
- Clarity in your thinking
- Healing in mind, body, and spirit
- Peace and awareness
- Empowerment to be all that you are created to be
- Acceptance and self-love
- Self-esteem
- Soul recognition of God's essence
- Loving and peaceful relationships
- Understanding and forgiveness
- Inspiration and enlightenment
- Gratitude
- The companionship of angels

- Release of blockages in your energy and physical body
- Release of trauma, stress, anxiety, worry, and negative thoughts and feelings
- Positive changes in your life and in the world
- The magnificence of who God is within you

CHAPTER TWO

What The Words "I Love Me" Represent

"I" Represents The Following:

- I choose to accept that God created me with love.
- I choose God's loving presence and essence within me.
- I choose God's light to illuminate my path.
- I choose to be all that God created me to be.
- I choose to have a soul connection to all that God is.
- I choose to rejoice in the glory of God.
- I choose God's abundant well-being in mind, body, and spirit.

- I choose the authority of God's power to call forth healing.
- I choose to be in harmony and peace with all of God's creation.
- I choose and express God's Divine power and love.
- I choose God's exuberant joy in my life.
- I choose God's wisdom and understanding for who I am.
- I choose God's enlightenment.
- I choose to walk in the presence of God and His angels.
- I choose to be connected to God's light.
- I choose to forgive, and to be forgiven.
- I choose to send forth love, and receive love.
- I choose to dispel all that is not of God's light back to God's light.
- I choose to be God's reflection of love, power and light.

"Love" Represents The Following:

- Love represents who you are as connected to God's presence.
- God's essence that is within you.
- Your acceptance of God's abundant love.
- Your choice to honor and love God.
- Your choice to honor and love yourself.
- God's exuberant joy and well-being for you.
- Your connection of oneness with God.
- Your connection to God's light.
- Your acceptance to create loving experiences.
- Your gratitude for being you.
- Your harmonious connection to all of God's creation.
- Your expression of love for God.
- The infinite love of God for you.

"Me" Represents The Following:

- You are God's creation.
- You are God's expression of love.
- You have a Divine connection to God.
- You are an expression of God's essence.
- You are a reflection and channel of God's light.
- You are in companionship with God.
- You are worthy of love.
- You have God's magnificence within you.
- You are Divinely created to know God's power.
- You are Divinely created to know joy.
- You are Divinely created to know happiness.
- You are Divinely created to know peace.
- You are Divinely created to know love.
- You are Divinely created to express the magnificence of who you are.
- You are in oneness with God who created you.
- You accept that you are loved.
- You walk in the presence of God and angels.

"I love me" represents all of this and more.

What Occurs When You Say *"I Love Me"*

When you say *"I love me"* you become part of and are connected to God's universal Divine energy for the manifestation of God's love in all manners and ways. Within this universal Divine energy is God's omnipresent power. It is this power that is within you. It is likened to being a seed that blooms into the beautiful flower it was designed to be. As you say *"I love me,"* you bloom forth into the magnificently created being God designed in you. When you say *"I love me,"* you enlist the Divine energy of powerful angels to align you with all the resources, people, and events to assist you in what you choose to do and become. The words *"I love me"* create a powerful vibrational connection with God's love. When you say *"I love me,"* you are choosing to connect with God's unwavering love and the power it brings forth. It represents your acceptance of all that God has designed for you.

The Power Of *"I Love Me"*

"I love me" is your acknowledgment that you have been created from God's love and you are accepting His love to release the flow of His power within you.

"I love me" is your soul's connection to love. In this connection, your eyes are opened to the understanding and vision of the majesty and magnificence of God within you.

"I love me" is your path to the victorious expression of the many gifts and capabilities created within you for your joyful and prosperous living.

"I love me" brings forth the love, laughter, joy, truth, knowing, wisdom, insight, and power of God's light flowing though you.

"I love me" brings forth a joyous state of being.

"I love me" can rule the consciousness of the world back to a loving and joyful state of being.

"I love me" can alter the energetic frequency by which the world takes form and can bring it to one of joyous harmony.

"I love me" in its very expression enlists the power and guidance of angels for the glorious expression of God in you.

"I love me" has been shared for its potency to bring changes of Divine magnitude.

"I love me" resonates with the magnificence of God's essence.

"I love me" can overcome negative energies or a bondage that blocks your connection to God.

"I love me" is a form of intuitive knowing that what you present to the world is a reflection of God's love and power.

"I love me" is the foundation to true inner knowing and love.

"I love me" is your connection to and acceptance of the power and love of God.

"I love me" is your communication with God to accept His wisdom and love for you.

As you voice *"I love me,"* you become the reflection of God's love and power. In this understanding of who you are and what you are designed to be, there is no acceptance of self-judgment, self-criticism, or self-hatred. When you say *"I love me,"* you allow for the fulfillment of the joyful and glorious you. When you say *"I love me,"* you fill every space within you with the essence of God's love, and there is no place for anything other than God's love. As you choose to say *"I love me,"* you choose to be a vessel for the power of God's love to flow throughout the universe.

As God's love flows from you into the universe, you become a source for God's light, which brings about healing changes. In choosing to be a source of God's light, your light can resonate with the light of others to bring love even in places where love seems not to exist. With this powerful proclamation of *"I love me,"* you are sending forth God's love and light to the hearts and minds of all whom God has created. As you do so, you shall abide in the love space, where God's love abounds.

When you say *"I love me,"* you surround yourself in the love space of God. You are likened to a painter who designs a masterpiece that reflects the expression of God's love. When you choose to be in the love space, you are designing a life that reflects God's masterpiece in the expression of His love within you. You are connecting to and gifting a part of God in you to others. As you abide in the love space, you allow for God's vibration of love to go forth to create changes within your life and within the world. In being the giver of God's light and love, your love space can magnify to the ends of the universe. In doing so, you bring those in your world to this higher state of God's love. The love that you send forth shall return the magnitude of God's light and love back to you. All who choose to love shall be in the love space of God.

God's love within each person has a profound effect upon the world when it is sent forth. The power of love can change the hearts and minds of people by awakening God's love within them. As you magnify the power of God's love through self-love, you elevate the energetic vibration and frequency of Divine love within the world. Your choosing to say *"I love me,"* can change the world by bringing forth God's love for harmony and peace. Sending forth the love of God within you creates a healing force in the world that overcomes hatred, resentment, anger, and the causes of war and strife. As you proclaim *"I love me,"* you bring others into the knowing and alignment with God's Divinity and healing love. We assure you that you can immediately affect change in any situation by saying *"I love me,"* and sending forth God's love. This proclamation has been Divinely given to show you how to be victorious in your life.

Where there is evil you can say *"I love me"* and love can go forth to dispel the evil.

Where there is hatred you can say *"I love me"* and love can go forth to bring forgiveness and unity.

Where there is hopelessness and despair, you can say *"I love me"* and love can go forth for the renewal of joy and laughter.

Where there is fighting and war between people, you can say *"I love me"* and love can go forth to bring peace and harmony.

Where there is loneliness, you can say *"I love me"* and love can go forth to bring comfort and compassion.

You have God's power in this moment to dispel anything not of God's love and light back to God's light. You have been given this authority, as God's essence is within you. There is no person or situation that can overcome God's love. You are being awakened to the truth that God's mighty power is within you. When you accept that you are connected to God's essence, you accept God's power that is within you to resonate love even to those you have never met. As you choose to love, you resonate love for the greater good of all in creation. Love then returns to you for all that you give is multiplied back to you. *"I love me"* is a powerful expression of how you can call forth God's love, light and power to affect your life and to have a resounding effect on the world.

The Joyful State Of *"I Love Me"*

Within your heart is God's abundant joy and it rises up within you when you say *"I love me."* The joy of who you are as Divinely created by God is what has been given to you as your inheritance. You have within you the wisdom that your life is designed for you to experience the joy of God's love. There are numerous possibilities for you to experience God's love. As you say *"I love me,"* you connect to and resonate with those possibilities to bring them into being.

Your angels come this day to enlighten you to the power that you have to create the experiences that bring love and the celebration of joy in God's presence. As you say *"I love me,"* you shall witness the magnitude of God's love in all forms. This is an awakening for you to know the truth of whom God is within you and the power of God's love to bring wisdom, joy and abundance into your life. As you choose this joyful state of being, your life experiences will reflect the treasures that God has designed for you.

When you choose to love and be loved, even in the midst of chaos or strife, you shall rise above that which attempts to steal your power and joy. Love elevates the power of your "aura" or the energy around you. It dispels the forces of evil and circles you in the glow of God's light. When you are in a state of love, you move beyond self-imposed limitations and fears. It brings

23

clarity to your thoughts for where there is love, there is a connection to Divine awareness and knowledge.

To bring yourself to a joyful state of being, you say *"I love me."* In your acknowledgement of the love of yourself, you resonate with God's Essence and it is there where abundant joy resides.

Ask yourself these questions to create an *"I love me"* joyful state of being:

- What am I grateful for in this moment?
- What am I joyful for in this moment?
- What expression of God's love am I in this moment?
- What expression of God's light am I in this moment?
- What expression of God's Divine power am I in this moment?
- What can I say, do, and be to reflect and experience God's essence, light and love in this moment?

As you ask yourself these questions, visualize God's Divine white light flowing upon and through you. Call upon your angels to send forth God's Divine wisdom to inspire you. In doing so, you can create an *"I love me"* state of being to experience and reflect God's expression of His love, joy, light and power within your life. When you say *"I love me,"* you align with the joy of God that is within you to create a joyful state of being.

CHAPTER THREE

God's Love Is Within You

What To Do When You Question The Love Of Yourself

There may be times in your life when you question the power of love or feel unloved. You may have fears, doubts and worries, or you may be experiencing illness and a lack of joy. It is during these times that you can choose to say *"I love me,"* and you can bring forth the power of God to assist you. God is within you and the choice to say *"I love me"* will bring positive changes to your life. It may happen in subtle ways at first, or you may even question if anything is occurring. Even though you may not have the awareness or evidence of what is being done for you in this moment, know that God's light and love are powerful. A change or turn in your situation may manifest instantly or occur over time. God has full knowledge of your path and where it leads. Choose to love yourself, and in doing so God's wisdom and path for your life will be revealed to you. You do not walk your journey in life alone. You always have God and His ministering angels with you. Call upon your angels and they will make God's love and power known to you.

When you say *"I love me,"* you are accepting all that occurs is in alignment with God's design for your life. It is as if a puzzle is being created where all the pieces fit together perfectly to form the grand picture. You may not have all the pieces arranged in your life puzzle yet, but they are being designed and will be put into place as God has designed them for you. When you say *"I love me,"* you empower the creation and coming together of all that is in the universe to fulfill what God has created within you.

Your Awareness That God Is Within You

The presence of God's love is always within and connected to you. You can, through your free will, disconnect from your knowledge of this truth; however, you cannot disconnect from God who brought you into being. If you have made choices to distance yourself from God's love, you can in this moment come back to the knowing and power of God's love for you by saying "*I love me.*" God's love is ever present within you. You have been designed and created in the image of God. The choice you make to love yourself brings forth the Divine awareness of God's presence within you. By loving yourself, you love God who is within you.

If you are in a place of unknowing, where you do not feel the presence of God within you, choose in this moment to accept the love of God for you. This important angelic message, that you cannot be disconnected from God, has great meaning in your experience. Even if you choose not to acknowledge God, or walk in a manner that is not an expression of God's love, your connection to God who created you remains. If you feel disconnected from, or are unsure of God's love for you, angels assure you that you always have the choice in each moment to accept God's love and to connect to God's light within you. When you say "*I love me,*" you connect to God's light and the abundant flow of God's love for you.

The Love Space

When you are in God's light where love abides, and say "*I love me,*" you are in the love space. In the love space, there is God's love and joy from which you were created. It is God's connection to you where love flows freely. When you choose to say "*I love me,*" you bring forth the joy of the love space where God's essence abides.

In the love space, there is a connection to all that God has created and you have the power to be in oneness with God. In the love space, there is no tolerance for any form of untruth that creates fear, worry, hatred, or any forms of bondage. There is no acceptance for anger or judgment toward yourself or others. God's presence of love overcomes such things. It is love that awakens the truth and the wisdom within you of the abundant power you have to be in oneness with God. True power comes neither from might nor by your position in life, but by the love of God within you. Accept the love of yourself and say *"I love me,"* for it shall bring the power of God's love space into your life.

It is a glorious day in the spirit world for angels are with you in the love space. They celebrate with joy the love God has for you. Angels have the authority to send forth God's light and love to meet your needs, bring joy to your life and to assist you in becoming all that God has created you to be.

The conjured notion that life is hard, and must be laden with challenges and troubles has infiltrated the minds of many people. Life is meant for celebration and the glorious expression of God's love. It is meant for the celebration of the joy of being you. Where there is suffering, despair, and hopelessness, God's love can be called forth to overcome such things. Angels as your companions enlighten you with the understanding of the power of God's love that comes from saying *"I love me."* Angels take great joy in sending forth and sharing God's love and light with you. There is a celebration among angels when you choose to love and you are in the love space.

You are created from God's love, and you have supreme importance in God's eyes. When you say *"I love me"* you are in the love space where you have the knowing of God's wisdom and power to affect your experiences in life. The veil of confusion or disbelief that keeps you from celebrating the joy of who you are, and may cause you to live in fear, can be lifted when you say *"I love me."* In the love space, love overcomes fear, and confusion is replaced with wisdom. In the love space, you are in the glow of God's light and the magnificence of who you are as a child of God shines forth. The love space is within you, for God is love and all that is of God is within you. When you receive and send forth love, you give glory and honor to God and you dwell in the love space. This is a time of rejoicing for as you choose to love yourself, you can experience the immeasurable joy of being in the love space.

God's Love And Light In The Love Space

Take a moment to quiet your mind and be still. Visualize the light of God flowing from the crown of your head through your heart and back to the crown of your head. You are now surrounded in the light where God and angels abide. Breathe in slowly for a count of five and breathe out slowly for a count of five. See yourself opening your heart space. Visualize God's exuberant love and joy flowing through you, filling every part of you with light and love, and then overflowing out into the universe. You are now surrounded in the love space. Angels are with you celebrating the joy of God's love. Repeat: "Thank you God, for your love within me. *I love me.*" And so it is.

CHAPTER FOUR

The Power In Choosing

In your connection to God's essence, what you choose has a resounding effect upon your experiences. You have been given free will in life, and God honors your free will and the choices you make. You can choose to accept God's love and power within you, and it shall be so. You can choose to call forth God's power through your words, and it shall be so. You can choose to call forth the love and guidance of angels, and it shall be so. Choosing to accept the love of God that is within you is choosing to be empowered.

Powerful "I Choose" Statements:

- I choose to say *"I love me."*

- I choose to receive and send forth love.
- I choose to be the expression of God's love.
- I choose to accept the love of God within me.
- I choose to accept God's power within me.
- I choose to be in oneness with God.
- I choose to be in the love space of God.
- I choose the power of God's essence within me.
- I choose God's infinite wisdom.
- I choose to accept and reflect the joy of who I am.
- I choose to be all that God is within me.
- I choose to be the magnificence of who God created me to be.
- I choose God's light to be upon me and to flow through me.
- I choose to walk in God's light.
- I choose to be surrounded by God's light.
- I choose the power of God's light.
- I choose the truth of God's light.
- I choose to expand my light in all directions for God's love and presence to be known.
- I choose to dispel anything not of God's light into the light.
- I choose to dispel fear, worry, and anxiety into God's light.
- I choose to accept the companionship, guidance and intervention of angels.
- I choose exuberant joy and laughter in my life.

- I choose to be a channel for God's peace.
- I choose peace of mind.
- I choose loving companionship.
- I choose peace and harmony in my relationships.
- I choose to have kind and loving friendships.
- I choose well-being.
- I choose healing in mind, body, and spirit.
- I choose to receive Divine awareness, clarity and truth.
- I choose to have comfort and joy wherever I am abiding.
- I choose to accept love and kindness.
- I choose to be abundant in all ways.
- I choose to resonate the power of God's light and love.
- I choose to be in oneness with all that is of Divine existence.
- I choose to be and reflect the magnificence of who I am.
- I choose to be in unity with God and angels.
- I choose to accept the wisdom and love of all that is of God.
- I choose to be in harmony with all of God's creations.
- I choose to be thankful for God's love and blessings in my life.
- I choose to be in gratitude.

- I choose to be protected, safe and relaxed in all my travels.
- I choose to have peace and joy in my family.
- I choose to work at a job that is rewarding and brings me joy and prosperity.
- I choose to love and honor God.
- I choose to love and honor who I am as a child of God.
- I choose God's abundant treasures designed for me.
- I choose to share God's love with all people.
- I choose my life to be a celebration of God's love and light.
- I choose to be that which I have spoken.

And so it is.

You Have Free Will To Choose The Manner In Which You Live

What you choose shall set into motion God's mighty power and the assistance of angels to bring all things into being.

Your life is not measured in days, but in expressions of who you choose to be.

You can choose to be free of man-made limitations and lack of any type.

You can choose to express the magnificence of who you are in countless ways.

You can choose to have abundance and all that brings forth joy.

God has given you free will to choose the manner in which you live. By choosing to love yourself, you are choosing to be free of man-made limitations. What you choose can set into motion God's mighty power and the assistance of angels to bring the magnificence of who you are into being. Through your choosing, you can open the flow of God's immeasurable wisdom to guide you on a path of victory in God's light. When you choose to say *"I love me,"* you call forth God's power and love to assist you in being the magnificent and joyful being you were created to be.

Choosing to say *"I love me,"* is a statement to the universe that you accept the love of God within you and all its possibilities for expression. Choosing love opens the door to more abundance in all ways. Choosing love turns on your light. In the light, which is God's presence, there is the knowing of well-being in mind, body, and spirit. What you choose in this moment is creating the expression of who you are. In your choosing to say *"I love me"* you align with the infinite Divine energy of the universe to become that which you choose.

Angels are with you to shine forth God's light and to help guide and support your choices. Angels can help change outcomes, supply resources and financial means, bring forth justice, open lines of communication, resolve disputes, give encouragement, remove doubt, fear and judgment, and open doors for your well-being that may have once seemed impossible to pass through. Angels can intercede for you to bring all things into existence for the expression of God's love.

You are the expression of what you choose. In your choosing, you can connect with God's love and light to bring forth God's power. You can bring forth experiences that exemplify God's love and joy. Choosing to say *"I love me,"* empowers that which you choose for the glory of God. Do not fall prey to the misguided view that there are powers in human form that control your destiny. There are no forces that have greater power in your life than God. As you choose to visualize the world through your connection to God's love, you immediately begin to send forth God's power to all in your human experience. You become a formidable force in the world with angels to assist you.

You are the vessel of God's love and light that beams stronger and brighter when you choose to say *"I love me."* All are under God's authority. When you choose to accept self-love, God's power is sent forth to bring insight, wisdom, and the resources for God's love to rule. Your vessel is being guided in God's light on a journey to experience God's love. You steer your vessel by the choices you make and God empowers your choices when you say *"I love me."* There may be some challenges or obstacles along your journey, but God and His angels are always with you guiding your path. Neither the forces of nature nor the forces of mankind shall have more authority in your life than God and His love for you.

Prayer Command To Send God's Love And Light To Others

"I call forth the love and light of God within me, and I send God's love and light forth to you. And so it is."

I Love Me Prayer For Choosing

You can choose to accept and become all that is of God within you through the *"I Love Me* Prayer for Choosing."

"I accept with gratitude that I am always at choice for the expression of who I am. I choose God's love, light, joy, wisdom, truths, enlightenment, power, and all that is of God's essence within me. I choose to be in oneness with God. *I love me*. And so it is."

As you become more enlightened of the grandeur of God's love for you, you will understand the potency that God's power and love have in your life. What you choose to say, do, or be will have a profound effect upon your life experience. You always have free will to choose to walk in the presence of God's light, and to surround yourself in the protection of God's light. You can do so by calling forth God's light around yourself, your family, your home, your community, and all in your world. In the light, there is God's love and there can be no darkness. When you choose to be in God's light, you are choosing to radiate God's love and power. In your choosing to be in God's light, you open the stream of God's power into your life, for the grandeur of God's presence to be witnessed.

When life presents to you a picture of anything not of God's love, you have the choice and the power to accept that you are a Divinely created being of love and light. Whatever is occurring not of love can be banished by you. You have authority to dispel and banish back to the light of God, everything not of God's light and love. When you do so, God's supreme wisdom and authority shall be in control. When you dispel something back to God's light, you relinquish its effects upon your life and God chooses what to do with it.

Prayer To Dispel Anything Not
of God's Love and Light

Speak to that which is not of God's light and love and say:

> "I now call forth God's love and light.
> Anything not of God's love and light,
> I dispel you. Return to the light.
> *I love me*. And so it is."

CHAPTER FIVE

Dispelling Anything Not Of God's Light

When you dispel that which is not of the light or of God's love, you put it within God's power to do as God pleases. You need not question or be concerned with what God chooses to do. You simply trust that what you dispel into the light is in God's control and it is no longer within your expression or experience. Dispelling anything not of God's light is a powerful proclamation. It is a means by which you can release and banish anything that tries to create fear or comes to steal the joy, love, or power within you. Choose to accept only that which is of God's light. When you do so, your life experiences will reflect God's power and love within you.

You have the authority within you to call forth the light, and to live your life free of that which distracts or hinders you from self-love. Voicing *"I love me,"* removes distracting thoughts that challenge your worthiness and self-love. When you say *"I love me,"* you accept God's love. You will not choose to criticize, judge, or make yourself less than who you are. You will be emboldened to call out fear and all negative thoughts and demand they return to God's light. If you have been misinformed or misguided to believe you are unworthy to receive God's love, awaken to the truth that you are worthy and God loves you.

As you choose to take up your power within God's light, you bring it forth into your existence. All creation is connected, and as you dwell in and send forth the light of God, it shall manifest love and healing in your life and in the lives of multitudes of people. In your connection to all creation, the love within you shall create love within others. Healing can go forth into the lives of people you have never met. Your choice to be in God's light can be like a candle that shines a light to people throughout the world. One person's light can illuminate the light of the masses. In doing so, you can bring the consciousness of others in the world to the vibrational healing energy of God's love. Saying *"I love me"* illuminates your light and goes forth to illuminate the light within others.

Your choosing to be in God's light is of great significance. When you choose to be and reflect God's light, you send forth God's love, which shall bring forth healing in all manners. In your connection to all creation, the love and joy within you can create love and joy within others. Simply by loving yourself and saying *"I love me,"* you bring forth God's light and love for the glory of God to be known. Choosing to be in God's light happens in the here and now. When you call upon them, angels align with you in what you are choosing to be, say, and do, and they empower whatever you choose. Choose to love yourself and say *"I love me,"* and you shall choose to be empowered in the presence of God's light.

Fear and all that is connected to fear has no power in God's light. It is an illusion that fear can harm you. Fear only takes on meaning when you dwell upon it, give it your attention, or give it your acceptance. When fear, worry, anxiety or negative thoughts rear their false illusions, you must take up your authority as a person connected to God's light and dispel them. They are powerless illusions, and with authority, you can banish them into God's light.

How To Release Fear

There may be times in your life when fear seems to pervade your thoughts or your experiences. Fear tries to dissuade you from knowing that you have God's power within you. It is during these times that you must take up a clear understanding of the reason for fear.

Fear is an attempt to blind you to how powerful you truly are. It presents a false image that you are powerless.

Fear attempts to have you focus on that which steals your joy and power.

Fear attempts to create chaos and confusion to disconnect you from your awareness of God's truths and wisdom.

Fear is likened to a bully that manipulates and intimidates you into thinking you have no choice but to succumb to its false illusions.

Fear only comes to persuade you to give away your power. Do not allow it to do so.

When you come into this type of fear that attempts to steal your joy and power, it is of the utmost importance that you understand you have authority over fear and all negative thoughts, energies, and feelings created from fear. You have power to dispel fear and all negative energies back to God's light. It is within God's light that fear and all lower negative energies are dispelled. Fear cannot exist within God's light. When you experience fear or anything else that challenges your joy and love, take up your authority and relinquish them to God's light. Surround yourself in God's light and visualize God's light beaming brighter and more powerful through you. See the fear and negative energies being dispelled into the light. When you do so, you shall be in your power.

A Powerful Command To Dispel Fear

"I now call forth God's love and light. Fear I dispel you. Return to God's light. *I love me*. And so it is."

You have God's authority to change the thoughts or views that create unwanted and undesirable thoughts and experiences. When you say *"I love me,"* it brings forth the love of God to overcome the thoughts and views that create fear and negative experiences. You are being reminded that fear is a manipulation by forces other than God to steal your power and joy. Do not allow fear to do so. You are connected to the light of God and you have God's power to banish fear and all that it creates. The proclamation of *"I love me"* dispels fear and brings forth the power of who you are created to be. Fear is the counter to love. When you say *"I love me"* you bring forth the love within you. As you do so, you bring about the power of God's love, which rules over fear, and all spiritual and human forces. All forms of lack, destruction, and fear are of the lower energy and can be banished in the presence of God's light when you say *"I love me."* Choosing to say *"I love me"* is your spiritual warfare to dispel and overcome fear and anything that is not of God's light.

God has designed you to be an expression of His love and power. You are forever connected to God's powerful love. By saying *"I love me,"* you acknowledge your acceptance of God's love and power to dispel fear. When you say *"I love me,"* you uplift and energize your consciousness, which can elevate the consciousness of those in your midst and within the world to a healing powerful state of love. Love overcomes fear and empowers you to walk in the joy of God's light.

What you do has an effect upon the world for all are connected through the light and love of God. Your light can go forth and bring to remembrance the light within others. In doing so, the light within the world rises to a higher vibration where love abides. Accept the love of God within you and you will be in the presence of God's light where there is power to dispel fear. And so it is.

Prayer For Calling Forth God's Light To Dispel Fear, Worry, Anxiety, Doubt And All Lower Energies

See God's light filling your entire being and say:

"Whatever or whoever is manifesting fear, worry, anxiety, doubt or any lower energy, I now call forth God's love and light and I dispel you. Return to God's light. You are no longer required, accepted, or needed here. Angels of light, remove these impostors. *I love me*. And so it is."

How To Release A Bondage Or Negative Influence

Life was designed for God's love to be revealed and experienced by all in creation. Each person has been given free will to choose to accept and to share God's love. In the midst of this allowance by a loving God, some choose not to accept God's love and to walk a path not of the light. In doing so, they may experience a bondage or a negative influence upon the body, mind or spirit. Any type of bondage can distance you from the love of God. You have the choice in each moment to accept the love of God and to release negative influences in your life. When you choose to love yourself and say *"I love me,"* you align with the power of God's light and love. In doing so, you can release the stronghold of any bondage or negative influence. You become the reflection of God's light. In the light, you have power to overcome any bondage or stronghold upon your life.

All that occurs is done under the watchful eye of God and nothing is missed. When you choose to accept and send forth God's love, it has a resounding effect upon the world and upon your life. Even those people who seek to keep others in bondage are affected by love and can change their point of view. When you choose and reflect love, the power of love can overcome the negative influences and bondages created in the world. All have God's light and love within and all have the choice to accept and reflect love. In every moment you are given the choice to love. The bondages and strongholds that distance you from God's love can be released by saying *"I love me."* When you say *"I love me,"* you are calling forth the power of God that is within you.

A Powerful Means To Release And Free Yourself Of A Bondage Or Stronghold

See the image of the world with its people in front of you.

See yourself standing in front of this vast world with all of its doctrines, thoughts, descriptions and preconceived ideas of how life is meant to be. See your inner light connecting to God's source of light. Visualize yourself locking into place your connection to God's light, and turning the switch to "On." As the light glows, be aware of it flowing though you and into the images in front of you. See all of the people and parts of your world being surrounded in the presence of God's illuminating light.

As the light goes forth, release into God's light all of the connections you have to false beliefs and doctrines, negative ideas, and bondages of mind, body and spirit. Release thoughts of fear, worry, and lack of any type. As your light expands and becomes more powerful, see everything in front of you being consumed by the light and getting smaller and smaller. You have freed yourself of bondages, misguided passed-down doctrines, negative thoughts and ideas, lower energies and false illusions of control and fear. Now, where you are, there is just the brightness of God's light. You are now walking in the illuminated light of God, connected to God's love.

You are in the light where there is freedom from bondages and anything not of God's love and light. You are beaming so very bright. As you beam your light, see yourself as the powerful and loved being that you are. You are connected to the flow of wisdom and knowledge of God. See the light embracing your choices and creating a path for you to realize them. You have chosen to be in the light, and now God's truth of who you are is being revealed to you. There are no fears, false doctrines, or controlling beliefs of what life should be. There is joy and abundant love. What is occurring in your life is guided by God's light and love. Your experience has been changed, and so too, all those in your midst have been changed.

You are free, floating in an effortless, blissful state of consciousness. Begin to acknowledge with gratitude your connection to God's source of light and love. It is in this space of love and light where the highest vibration of Divine power comes into being. Impostors like fear, anxiety, depression, confusion, despair, worry, doubt and hopelessness are dispelled. Begin to voice the power of the words *"I love me."* There will be rejoicing when you do so, for you are acknowledging the love and power of God within you that sets you free. It is God's love that is the true source of power and brings forth the expansion of abundance, peace, and prosperity within your life. It is the power of God's love that gives you the freedom to be the magnificent creation you are designed to be. Raise your hands and call forth your acceptance of God's love through the people, experiences, and angelic beings that He is now sending to you on your journey. God's abundant love and light is upon you. And so it is.

CHAPTER SIX

What The Proclamation Of "I Love Me" Brings Forth

The proclamation of *"I love me"* brings forth God's light, love and wisdom for you to know how infinitely loved you are, and the power of God within you to create joy, happiness, well-being and abundance in your life. The proclamation of *"I love me"* can dispel fear, anxiety, and anger. It can bring forth healing and harmony to your relationships. It can burst forth the magnitude of God's presence in a manner you have not imagined or seen.

When you say *"I love me,"* you abide with the divinity of God and Christ's Spirit of love.

"I love me" connects people of all walks of life and beliefs through God's love and light. When you

say *"I love me,"* you bring forth God's love into the world for harmony and unity between people. Even though there are differences in thoughts and beliefs among people, God's love is the same. When you say *"I love me,"* and walk in God's love, there is no need for fighting for control, power, and authority among people, for it is truth that God creates all equally. When you say *"I love me,"* and you choose to send forth God's love, you need not challenge the beliefs of others or be challenged for your beliefs. God's light and love shall bring understanding and acceptance.

Power Comes From God's Essence And Love Within You

The more you choose to love you and say *"I love me,"* the greater your power will be. There is no need to force your values, opinions, ways of thinking, or desires upon anyone or have them forced upon you. You merely accept and send forth God's light and love, and God will do the rest. Life becomes one of joy when you accept that God is the master planner of all life and is in control of all that exists.

Your life is designed by God and you are under the protection of God's love. You have within you the knowing that you are connected to God. It is through this connection to God's light and love that connects you to all of creation. When you choose to say *"I love me,"* you send forth God's love to create healing within your life and within the lives of people you may never have met. You have God's power to create your life experiences and to release anything not of God's light and love. God is always with you and guiding your path. He sends angels to assist you and to reveal His power to you. It is your choice to say *"I love me,"* and to accept and send forth the love of God.

All people are created through God's essence of love and light, and all people are equal in this manner. Everyone is given free will. Through your free will you can choose to express the power of God's love and light. Some may choose to fall prey to the false belief that power is determined by your position or status in life. When you accept this truth that God's power is within you, you will understand that your power is not based on human standards. God is the true source of all power and He has authority over all that exists. There is no force or power greater than God's love within you. When you choose to say *"I love me,"* it brings forth the power of God's love, which rules over all that is and that will be. Each time you say *"I love me,"* it empowers you and has immediate effects upon your life and upon the rest of the world.

When you choose to act in a manner that does not express love toward yourself or others you distance yourself from the power of God's love and light. You can choose to accept and empower your connection to God's love and light by saying *"I love me."* You were created by a loving God who chose to shine forth His light through you. You were created to be in companionship with God and angels. You were created to be in harmony with all of God's creations. You were created to know joy and to walk in God's light. You were created to be in oneness with God and to be the expression of His love. God is the creator of love and has a connection within all people to His love. Each person has been given free will by God and can choose to accept God's love and walk in His light. God has full knowledge of what is inside each person's heart.

He knows everything about you. If you are in a place where you are unsure of God's love for you, or you are acting in a manner that is distancing you from God's love, you can in this moment accept God's love by choosing to say *"I love me."* The moment you do so, God will send forth His light and love upon you. When you choose to love, there is rejoicing among angels as they joyfully guide you on your life's journey.

Choosing to love yourself and saying *"I love me"* can bring healing into your life and into the world. The path you walk has many opportunities for you to experience and reflect God's love. The love of God can bring forth healing to the mind, body, and soul. The love of God can bring forth joy, inner peace and love within your heart. The love of God can put an end to fighting and wars among people. The love of God can calm the forces of nature and protect you from harm. All have a knowing of God's light and love within them. All have a role in creating peace and harmony. You always have the choice to accept God's love. You always have the choice to follow the path of God's light. You can choose to send forth the power of God's love and light into any situation. You have God's wisdom and power within you to inspire you and guide your way. You have the opportunity in every moment to choose and experience the power of God's love in your life. You can do so by saying *"I love me,"* and by choosing to love. The importance of this angelic message of expressing *"I love me,"* is given to all people. The choices you make now create your present and future life experiences. You can create a life filled with joyful and loving experiences by choosing to love and by saying *"I love me."*

We come to share this truth that the love that is within you connects you to God and to all creation. When you say *"I love me,"* you send forth God's love and light into the world. When you express *"I love me,"* there is no judgment of you or others. There is just this love connection where God's love and light flow freely. In the presence of God's love, you can immediately affect your experiences and the experiences in the world. It is through love that you accept your own Divine connection. God's wisdom and truths are stored within the soul consciousness of each person. By saying *"I love me,"* God's wisdom and truths are made known to you. God gives each person countless reminders of His love and power. He sends angels to inspire you and to intervene on your behalf. You have the choice to reflect God's love and light and to remind others of God's love and light within them. You are part of a circle of love with God, angels, and your fellow human beings. When you choose to say *"I love me,"* you open your heart to receive the love of God, your angels and your fellow human beings.

Some may question the power of self-love and the importance of proclaiming *"I love me."* We assure you that the power of self-love is and has always been within your knowing. Your worthiness to say *"I love me"* is because God's essence and love are within you. When you love yourself, you love and honor God who created you. When you say *"I love me,"* you bring forth God's unwavering love and power that is within you. Accepting and sharing God's love is your choice in every moment. If you choose to do so, your life can unfold in miraculous ways beyond what you can imagine.

Through God's power, you can become the light that stills the darkness.

Through God's power, you can call forth healing.

Through God's power, you can align with angels to bring harmony and peace in the world.

You can experience and be a reflection of God's love and power when you choose to share all of the gifts, talents and wisdom that God has instilled within you. As you voice *"I love me,"* you will gain God's insight and see the signs of its effects upon your experiences. The meaning and importance of self-love that is being shared through these angelic messages is, that in loving yourself, you love and give honor to God who is within you. The proclamation *"I love me"* is a proclamation of *"I love God."* For to love yourself, whom God created, is to show appreciation and love for God who is in you.

Self-love aligns you with the love of God. It brings the love of God's presence and healing power into your life and into the world. Self-love is a way that you can express God's presence within you to the world. It gives you the freedom to be what God created you to be. It awakens and connects you with the love of God within you to bring to your awareness the magnificence of who you are and what you can become. When you say *"I love me,"* you become absorbed in the exuberant love of God. When you say *"I love me,"* you are acknowledging God created you and His presence is instilled within you. When you say *"I love me,"* you are accepting your worthiness as a child of God, created in His image to express His love.

We come to enlighten all to this awareness of God's essence and love that is within you. We come to empower you to look at life through the eyes of love. In your loving vision of the world, there is a vibrational energy that you send forth that connects with the Divine energy of God's love. Through this connection, you have the allegiance of God's angels who come to minister to you. You have the choice in every moment to be a reflection of God's love and light. You can overcome lower and negative forms of energy that come to take from you what God has designed for you and is rightfully yours, by choosing to love and by saying *"I love me."*

CHAPTER SEVEN

Walking In God's Light

God's light is upon and within you. Within God's light
there is a celebration of the love of God. As you choose
to say *"I love me,"* you allow for the resonance of
God's all-consuming light and love to pervade your
world. Nothing can supersede the power of God's love
and light. God will never flounder in any manner in
His love for you. He will never turn His back upon
you. He is forever with you. You have within you an
understanding and knowledge of this truth that sets
you free and enlivens you to victorious and glorious
living. God is love, and His love is always and forever
within you. God sends forth His light to bring you
an understanding of His love and the power of His
presence.

Connecting with God's light and love is your choice. You simply choose, and God will do the rest. When you choose to love yourself and you say *"I love me,"* you are choosing to accept God's light and love. Within the light, there is a knowing of God's essence that is within you. There are no forces, energies, or forms of darkness that can overcome your choice to say *"I love me"* and the power it brings. *"I love me"* is a proclamation that can overcome fear, unknowing, darkness and lower energies. Self-love connects you to God's love and is a powerful means by which you create peace, harmony, and joy in your life and in the world. It is a means by which you become a part of the celebration in the light with angels who rejoice with you.

The Meaning Of God's Light

- God's light is an expression of and connection to God's love and power that exists within all creation.
- God's light has the power to bring forth love, healing, protection, wisdom, and all of the treasures of God.
- God's light is given with authority to angels.
- God's light is radiant, vibrant, peaceful, and joyful.

- God's light is a source of God's love, presence, and power, and all that is created by God.
- God's light rules over mankind and all forces in life.
- God's light holds the destiny for the creation of life.
- God's light brings forth the power of God's unwavering love and wisdom.
- God's light contains God's essence.
- God's light is within you.
- In God's light there is celebration for the presence of God.

Powerful Proclamations In God's Light

In the light, there is love and a connection to God's essence. Send forth God's light around everything you have now and everything that is in the future. Dwell not on the things that cause you anguish or fear. Choose only to be an expression of God's light. It is within God's light, that all power flows forth for you to be the expression of God's love. There is unfathomable joy when you walk in God's light and proclaim the power of the light in what you choose.

The Following Are Powerful Proclamations For You To Say:

- I choose to say *"I love me."*
- I choose to be loved.
- I choose to accept God's light.
- I choose to be powerful.
- I choose to be joyful.
- I choose to be happy.
- I choose to be empowered.
- I choose to be peaceful.
- I choose to be well.
- I choose to be in the knowing.
- I choose to be healed.
- I choose to be calm.
- I choose to be magnificent.

- I choose to be abundant.
- I choose to be forgiving.
- I choose to be confident.
- I choose to be inspired.
- I choose to be a vessel of God's power and light.
- I choose to be free of bondages
- I choose to be in God's presence.
- I choose to be in the company of angels.
- I choose to be courageous and strong.
- I choose to be victorious in life.
- I choose to be enlightened.
- I choose to be a child of God.
- I choose be Christ's spirit of love.
- I choose to be in oneness with God.

We acknowledge that there are moments when you may question the power of these proclamations in your life, but as you stay true to them, you will form experiences in tune with their Divine vibrations.

This information is being shared to bring forth the ever-present power of God's light and love. The stories of woe presented by some as a way of life do not exist when you are in the light. Within God's light there is power, joy, abundance, and healing. *"I love me"* is your proclamation to be in God's light and to be a witness of God's omnipresent power and love.

Celebrating With Angels In The Light

Angels send forth God's rays of peace and exuberant joy. They assure you that you are loved. You are the gift that has been wonderfully created by the love of God. You share your gift with others when you choose to say *"I love me."* When you speak *"I love me,"* you release God's light and love to bring healing to yourself and to the world. In their love for you, angels guide you to know the power of God within you, and how to release fears and anything else that distances you from God. They come to bring to your awareness the power of who you are, and what you can do and become. Angels celebrate in God's light when you choose to love and be loved.

Angels are your companions, and when you rejoice, they rejoice with you. Their love is ever present. There are no limits to what angels can do for you, for God is their source of unlimited power and insight. Angels send messages through people and events that cross your path, to assure you that you are being guided in God's light. You will feel their presence uplift your spirit and enlighten you with thoughts of inspiration. They will inspire words of wisdom in your communication with others and lead you on the path to reach your goals. Their assistance is Divinely given and can come in all ways and manners. All that is created within the universe is at their service. They can open doors that were once closed, move roadblocks that seem unmovable, bring insight where there appears to be no resolution, and send people to assist you and guide you safely on your journey.

Angels see what is not always within your view or understanding. They know which path will lead to your desired end, even when that path may seem to be filled with obstacles. The obstacles you view as troublesome, the angels see as stepping-stones to your victory. The all-knowing and greater view of where a path may lead comes from God's wisdom, which angels have awareness of. When you are being guided to take a course that your human understanding finds questionable, ask for the assistance and insight of your angels. All knowledge is within you for which path to take and angels shall bring this knowledge to your awareness. Angels are sent as your guides and when you ask, they will assist you with the choices you make. They will guide you through God's light on a golden path to know God's love. There is power in saying *"I love me,"* because that brings awareness. It calls forth Divine intercession to reveal God's truths and removes the doubts, and concerns that clutter the mind and hinder your progress.

Angels celebrate with you in the presence of God's light. In the vision of a human being, God's light sometimes appears to be hidden beneath the cares of the day. When you choose to say *"I love me,"* God's light and love shall go forth to overcome the concerns and bondages that have weighed you down. Through the power of God's love and light, you shall have freedom from the chains created by human thoughts, fears, and actions. God's light removes the darkness and awakens you to the power of His love. It is within the light of God that there is a celebration by angels for the presence of God's love being made known through you.

Angels come to celebrate with you in your knowing of the truth that God's light and love are within you always. They celebrate the joy of who you are and the love that comes in your acceptance of God's love. The moment you say *"I love me,"* there is a celebration among angels for you. Ask your angels to walk with you and converse with you on your journey. It is with exuberant joy that they will do so as they celebrate in God's light, the love and companionship they have with you.

Prayer To Accept Your Connection To God's Light, Love And Power

I am Divinely created by God. I accept my connection to God's source of light, love and power. I dispel and return all that is not of

God's light, love and power back to God's light. I choose to be in oneness with God.

"I Love Me."

And so it is.

CHAPTER EIGHT

Your Connection To God And Angels

You are a reflection of God's love. Within you is God's DNA. It holds the love of God for you to connect with the magnitude of God's love, light and power in all manners and forms. The more you choose to say and confirm *"I love me,"* the stronger this connection and the fulfillment of God's DNA within you becomes. Within God's DNA is abundant joy, love, wisdom, and likeness to all that God is. You are the reflection of God, and all that is of God is within you. Through your knowing and acceptance of the presence of God's DNA, and His essence within you, you receive the power and abundant flow of God's love. You can choose to be an expression of God's DNA and abundant love in what you experience in each moment.

God's love has been brought forth in human form for God chose to dwell within you. By saying *"I love me,"* you bring forth God's Divine grace, Divine love, Divine truth, Divine wisdom, and all the treasures of God that are within you. As you say *"I love me,"* all that is stored within God's DNA can blossom forth for you to be the reflection of God's unwavering love and power.

Angels Are With You Always

Angels come to shift your thinking from a state of human concerns and worries to one of love, joy and freedom. They are forever by your side and can take on earthly form, if need be. Angels are your companions, the bringers of joy and wisdom. They have been given the role by God to love, guide, and enlighten you with the power of God within you.

Angels take joy in walking your journey with you. When you succumb to the world's view that often rules by fear, you distance yourself from the knowing of the power of God within you. Angels come to remind you to dispel your fears to God's light. They remind you of the power of God's love that is within you, and of your Divine connection to God. At any time, you can choose to call upon and converse with your angels. They will enlighten you to who you truly are and the power of God's love for you. There are times when angelic assistance comes when you have not consciously asked for assistance because your inner soul consciousness is doing so. When you say *"I love me,"* you empower your soul consciousness to request and accept the love and power of God and the assistance from angels.

When the angels gave the awareness of the importance of sharing the power of *"I love me,"* the spirit of truth went forth to align all who chose to accept and share in it. You have chosen to know and receive the awareness of these Divinely given angelic messages, for this is how this knowledge has come to you. As an infinite being, you have a wealth of God's knowledge, truth, and wisdom within you. You can allow the revelation of this knowledge to flow by being in the state of self-love and by choosing to love. As you absorb this knowledge, you will awaken to a glorious knowing of the power of God's love that exists throughout the universe.

Angels are in the midst of where you are in this moment. You can ask them to give you clarity and understanding, and they will do so. As you converse with your angels, your experiences will reflect Divine and angelic assistance. You have within you a storehouse of wisdom and information beyond all that you know. When you say *"I love me,"* you allow for the flow of this information to awaken you to all that

God has created and designed for you. This storehouse of wisdom can reveal God's truths, which can teach and guide you how to live a joyful and empowered life.

Your Importance And Worthiness As A Child Of God

Reflect upon these questions:

Do you know that you are worthy of God's love?

Do you know how much you are loved?

Do you know that your life is of extreme importance?

Do you know that healing is within you?

Do you know that your life is meant for joyful celebration?

Do you know that your path is lined with angels to assist you?

Do you know that in this moment, you have the power to affect your life to reflect God's love that is within you?

The good news is God wants you to know and experience all of the above! By loving yourself, you open the flow of God's abundant love, wisdom and treasures for you. As you honor and love yourself, your experiences change to align with the worthiness of who you are as a child of God. Worthiness is not based on human standards or beliefs, your place in life, or what you do or do not have. Worthiness comes from the understanding that God chose you and created you from His love. You are worthy because God created you! You are worthy because God loves you! You are worthy because you are part of God's family! As His creation, you inherit all that is designed for you in the kingdom of God. You are being reminded to accept your place in God's family and to walk in the presence of the love of your Father that is ever present with you. As God's Divinely created and abundantly loved child, you have a direct connection to God. That connection is always within you. Angels come to awaken you to this truth that God abides within you. You have access to God's love and wisdom in every moment of your life. When you converse with God and seek His wisdom, He hears you and He always responds. His response comes in many ways. He calls forth His ministering angels and others in your life to assure you of His presence, and to assist you in meeting your needs. Know that you are worthy of God's love and walk as a child of God. Begin by saying "*I love me.*" By giving your acceptance to love yourself, you accept the love of God within you and your place in the family of God. There is nothing greater than the love of God for you.

An Angel Hug To Uplift And Encourage You

Sit quietly and imagine yourself in the arms of an angel with God's love and light surrounding you. Visualize handing over to your angel all fearful, worrisome, negative and misguided thoughts about yourself. Hand over any thoughts you have of being unworthy to be loved. Dwell upon God's love and light to fill every part of your being. See yourself in God's loving presence with angels welcoming you. Allow the light of your angel to surround you and embrace you with love. Say, "Thank you God for loving me and for my angel hug." You have received the loving embrace of your angel assuring you of God's love and your worthiness as His child.

CHAPTER NINE

Abundance, Prosperity And Well Being

You have a Divine companionship with God, who is the source of all love and abundance. Within the kingdom of God there is no lack of any type. There is a bountiful supply of all that God has created for your joy and well-being. It is the love within you that holds the bountiful supply of all that God has created for you. When you say *"I love me,"* you are accepting your place in the kingdom of God where love and the bountiful supply of all God created for you flow freely and endlessly. It is God's never-ending supply of love that brings forth your abundance in mind, body, and spirit, and in all manners in your life.

As you choose to love yourself, you connect with God's never ending supply of love that brings all things into being. As your love expands, so too does your energetic Divine vibration. It is as if you send out a Divine signal that you are choosing to accept God's abundance and love and it is being manifested for you. Choosing to love yourself and say *"I love me"* is your confirmation that you are open to receive the expansion of love, abundance and well-being in all areas of your life. It allows God's love to go forth, creating experiences that reflect the joy and love within you. Choosing to love and be grateful for who and what you are brings forth God's abundant supply of love and the treasures it holds.

Love Brings Forth God's Healing Power For You

Angels come to remind you of God's love and the free will you are given to choose all that God's love brings forth. They take great joy in helping you to experience the many treasures God has created for you. The treasures of God's love can be experienced in countless ways. It can bring forth joy in your spirit, love in your relationships, healing in your family, abundance in your living, well-being in mind, body and spirit, peace in the world and much more.

This proclamation, *"I love me"* has profound power. In your choosing to say *"I love me,"* you connect with the flow of God's treasures, which are ever present and never ending. Choosing to love yourself and saying *"I love me"* allows God's love to go forth, creating experiences that reflect God's presence and love for you. When you choose to be an expression of God's essence and love, you experience angelic intervention in your life. Through God's power, angels can assist you in experiencing healing, joy, love, laughter and peacefulness along your journey.

Within you is God's love and healing power that are connected to all the treasures designed for you. When you say *"I love me,"* you accept your connection to God's source of all love and healing power. When the physical body experiences illness, remind it of God's love and healing power and call it forth. See yourself surrounded in God's love and light and see it filling every part of your being. Send God's love to the part of you that is experiencing illness or discomfort. Remind it of its connection to God's source of love and healing power. Repeat, *"I love me."* Do not be persuaded that your illness is a sacrifice you make for God, or has been sent to you by God. Rather, dispel anything not of your well-being back to God's light. Ask for God's healing power and wisdom to guide your way, and to bring angels and people into your life to assist you. Be of joy, for God who is within you can do mighty works through you.

Prayer To Bring Forth Physical Healing

"I accept and call forth the power of God's love for healing of mind, body and spirit. I accept the love of God within me to relinquish any causes of illness and discomfort. Body, I remind you that God's love is within me and your role is to manifest abundant health and well-being. Anything not of this well-being, I dispel back to God's light. *I love me*. And so it is."

God's Decrees

A decree of God is a solemn promise of God of your worthiness to experience His love and power.

In God's decrees, all are loved and all have the power to be an expression of His love.

In God's decrees, all are formed in the image of God and all have God's authority to send forth His light and love for healing.

In God's decrees, you can create life experiences of peace and harmony.

In God's decrees, you are designed for the awareness and expression of God's love, power, and joyful living.

In God's decrees, the knowing of God's truths is instilled within each soul consciousness.

In God's decrees, you are the reflection of His power and love.

God's decrees are ever present when you seek God's wisdom and choose to love.

There is an inner dialogue between you and God that brings forth the wisdom of who you are, and the power of God's love and light within you. When you say *"I love me,"* you are expressing acceptance and gratitude for God's decrees.

You are designed for the awareness and expression of God's love, power, and joyful living. Thoughts of illness, fear, destruction, and lack of any type are thoughts of untruth that are put forth to control, steal, and inhibit your power. It is only when you accept these untruths as the expression of your existence that they take on form and meaning. Do not choose to accept these thoughts of untruth. They are impostors that come to steal what is rightfully yours. You have God's power to overcome such things. It is not by might that you overcome the lower energies and the forces of untruth, but by the power of God's love within you. You can banish anything not of God's light by choosing to dispel it back to God's light. That is the power you have within you.

Angels come to share this important knowledge that the time for you to choose who and what you shall be is now, in the present. Situations may cause you to succumb to the acceptance or belief that you do not have control over your life. This, too, is an untruth, for it is in your choosing that you create your life's path and your life's journey. You have the power through God's love and light to create and change your experiences.

The Importance Of Removing Clutter In Your Thoughts

Clutter in your thoughts is caused by lower energies that create fearful or negative thoughts. You may experience clutter as voices in your head or an endless flow of confusing or worrisome thoughts telling you untruths about yourself, or others in your life. Clutter in your thoughts come to steal your joy and power. Thoughts that create clutter and consume the mind with worries, anxieties, and fears are lower forms of energy. These thoughts attempt to convince you that you are less than who and what you are. You may at times take on these untruths by accepting descriptions of who you are by those who are misinformed or do not see you as God sees you. People who you love, trust, or respect may pass on advice and ideas that create confusion, self-judgment, fear, and feelings of unworthiness. You may accept a view within the world that attempts to portray life as fearful and unfair. Whatever the source of these thoughts of clutter, you have the choice and the power to remove them from your life.

You can choose to remove and dispel to God's light all deceptive and unruly thoughts that create clutter in your mind and attempt to steal the love, joy and power that is rightfully yours. Thoughts that create clutter only have the power that you give to them. They are not real and cannot harm you when you remind them of God's power and love within you, and dispel them to God's light. Put your thoughts in God's control by loving yourself and saying "*I love me.*" The thoughts that create clutter in your mind will cease. They will have no power to cause you fear or harm. When you choose to love yourself, and accept God's love, clutter in your thoughts is replaced with the power of God's love to create a loving and joyful life for you.

You are created for the celebration of life with all of its joy and magnificence. Your thoughts can be the reflection of God's view of you as His magnificent creation. This is a moment for rejoicing, for you are being enlightened about the importance of removing clutter in your thinking. The means by which you can do so is by saying "*I love me.*" As you call forth God's light and repeat "*I love me,*" there will be no space for the harmful effects of clutter in your thoughts or experiences.

Angels are sharing this powerful message to assist you in creating joyful and loving experiences in your life. Some may question why there is so much evidence of things that create a lack of joy in life. The words of wisdom being shared here are for all to know the power you have within to create joyful living. The false beliefs that have been taught, inherited, or learned, thus creating an unhappy or harmful existence, must be dispelled to God's light. Choose not to accept such beliefs even if the consciousness of the world is presenting them as reality or fact.

God's essence of love that is within you and within all of creation has power over all that exists. Angels are sharing this powerful message of saying *"I love me,"* to assist you in experiencing God's essence of love and creating joyful and loving experiences in your life. Angels send forth rays of God's light to remove fear and bondages in mind and spirit. They bring clarity to your thinking to remind you how loved and powerful you are, and how you can experience God's love and peace in your life. Speak to the thoughts of clutter in your mind and banish them into God's light. Seek and ask for God's peace of mind and joy to be made known to you. Ask your angels for assistance and it will be so.

What To Do When You Experience Lack In Your World

When there appears to be lack in your life, begin by giving thanks and having gratitude for who you are as a child of God. There is always something to be grateful for. You can be grateful for being Divinely created and having God's light upon you. You can be grateful for God's love and presence in your life. You can be grateful for angels who abide with you. You can be grateful that this message of the power of saying *"I love me"* has been brought to your awareness. You can be grateful for being magnificently you! When you give thanks and express gratitude, you align with the Divine universal vibration and energy of God's love that is the source of all abundance. It is through your gratitude and thankfulness that you can bring forth God's abundance in your life. God's abundance comes in many forms and ways. To be truly abundant is to know and experience God's love for you, and to share God's love with others. When you accept the love of yourself and give love to others, you experience the highest form of God's abundant love and all that it brings forth. When you experience lack of any form, remind yourself of your connection to God's love from which all abundance flows. Do not listen or dwell upon the woes of the world or accept that experiencing lack in your life is unavoidable. When you repeat the words

"I love me," you are accepting the love of God for you, and you are accepting all that God has designed for your abundance in mind, body and spirit.

What if you make your requests known and it seems as if nothing changes? What if you continue to see signs of lack in your life and in the world? It is then that you say *"I love me"* and you continue to do so. You are confirming your love for God and it is God who meets all of your needs.

Prayer To Call Forth The Power Of God's Abundance

"I am aligned with God, the source of all that is, and I call forth God's abundance in my life. Anything not of God's abundance, I dispel and return to the light. I am one with God. *I love me*. And so it is."

The choices you make affect your life experiences and the world around you. You may not have the awareness in this moment of the profound changes occurring within your experience through the choice to say *"I love me,"* but changes are occurring. You may not immediately see with your eyes such changes, but rest assured that your life experience is changing. Your choice to say *"I love me"* brings forth the power and love of God's presence, and it goes forth to create experiences that reflect God's love. When you choose to say *"I love me,"* you are choosing to accept God's love, power and Divine abundance to be reflected in your life experiences.

You are the creation of a mighty God whose loving presence overcomes any and all forms of lower energies. You now have the proclamation of *"I love me"* to dispel anything that challenges your power or brings lack in any form. You are created to be the expression of God's love. If you are experiencing or sensing a lack of connection to God's love for you, or lack of any type within your life, take this moment to choose God's abundant love to overcome such things. Begin by saying *"I love me,"* and give gratitude to God for His unwavering love for you.

What you choose goes forth and has a resounding effect upon what you experience. You can choose to believe in God's love and power, and it will be so. You can choose to have angels line your path, to bring forth events and circumstances for your well-being, and it will be so. God honors your choice to love yourself, which creates new and loving experiences. His love never ceases for you. God's love is ever present and can overcome your doubts, fears, and any form of lack. You are the reflection of God's love and you have immeasurable power to call forth God's love into your life experiences. Whatever your position or place in life, you can manifest new and more loving experiences. Loving yourself is a choice that brings forth your Divine inheritance. In each moment there is the seed of life waiting to burst forth with God's inheritance for you.

Life is a presentation of the magnitude of God's endless blessings and opportunities to express His Divinity within you. As you say *"I love me,"* you accept the love of God within you that holds all His treasures for you. It is God's desire for you to express the loving essence of who you truly are. It is God's desire for you to receive your Divine inheritance that holds God's love for you. The proclamation of *"I love me"* is your acceptance of all the love, joy, treasures and blessings God had designed for you. Choose to say *"I love me"* and you shall experience God's abundant love for you.

The Time For Awakening

You are being awakened to the power of God's essence and love that inhabits who you are. When you say *"I love me,"* you will experience shifts in your thinking and in the life experiences that you have. You shall bring forth God's power to rise above the obstacles in your life and affect the world around you. There are no mountains that are insurmountable. Love is the most powerful force in the world, and when there is love there is God's presence. The more people, who choose to love, the greater will God's light shine forth to all corners of the universe. In doing so, the magnitude of God's power shall be seen.

You can affect the world in this moment by loving yourself, which brings forth God's love. God's love creates peace and joy. It overcomes hatred and any plans for destruction or harm. Cover your homes, places of work, schools, churches, and the like with the words *"I love me,"* as a symbol of God's love for and protection over you. You can do this by speaking the words *"I love me,"* and by posting them for all to read. It is the Divine energy of these words that brings forth the power of God's love and light. Make this commonplace in all that you do. You will experience God's loving presence.

CHAPTER TEN

The Power That Comes From Loving Yourself

There is power that comes from loving yourself. When you proclaim *"I love me,"* you create a Divine vibration within the universe, and God's love and presence is made known. In God's presence, there is the magnitude of power that formed the universe. This same power is within you and expressed when you love yourself. Saying *"I love me"* aligns you with the magnitude of God's power, which created the universe. It lifts the consciousness of the world to the acceptance of God's love. Each time you say *"I love me,"* you are sending forth God's love and the effect upon your life and the world is immeasurable.

When you say *"I love me,"* you love and honor God. It creates a Divine expansion of God's love and light that flows out into the universe. Where there is God's light, there can be no darkness. Angels come to encourage and support your choice to be the loving expression of God's love. They know the blissful joy that God's love brings and the power that comes from loving yourself. Angels are sent to share this blissful joy with you. In each moment there is a seed within you of God's infinite love and Divine possibilities to be all that you are created to be. You have the choice to water your seed by loving yourself. You can choose God's love and power in your life, and it shall be so.

There is a Divine spiritual vibration within these three words *"I love me."* The mere thought of these words can raise your consciousness for experiencing God's love. As you choose to say *"I love me,"* God's wisdom and love are made known to you. You shall have the knowledge of who God is and the power that His love brings forth. You become one with God from whom all of creation comes into being. You are likened to the power of a pebble cast into the ocean that creates a ripple effect that can bring changes to an entire ocean. When you love yourself, you release love into the world that can change your life experiences, and the entire world. The love you send forth can have a ripple effect that opens the hearts and minds of people in the universe to create a peaceful and loving existence.

The Love and Power of *"I Love Me"*

"I Love Me" Means:

- You love God, who is within you.
- You abide in God's presence and light.
- You are expressing your acceptance of God's Divine power.
- You are choosing to be the Divinely created you.
- You are choosing to be in oneness with God's power, love and wisdom.
- You are choosing to accept all that is of God within you.
- You are choosing to bring forth experiences that reflect God's love.
- You are choosing to elevate the presence of love in the world.
- You are resonating the magnificence of God's love.
- You are choosing a joyous state of being.
- You are choosing to be in God's light.
- You accept that your life is of extreme importance.
- You accept the love of God and His truths for what He created in you.
- You are sending out a powerful vibration of love that has an effect upon your life and the consciousness of the world.

You shall experience many signs of God's love in your life. His love may come in ways that lift your spirit, bring you exuberant joy, enlighten your mind, heal your body, and fulfill your needs. The endless flow of assistance may come in the way of angels and people who have been given direction by God to do so. In the midst of challenges or obstacles, keep your attention on the power of God within you. God's ray of light has the power to shine forth to illuminate your path and guide you on your journey. God's love is always with you, and He gives authority to His ministering angels to supply you with the means to be victorious.

Each person receives God's treasures as their inheritance. These treasures are filled with God's essence, wisdom, love and power. It is your choice to accept God's treasures that are designed for you, and to express God's love in who you choose to be and what you choose to do. As you say *"I love me"* and acknowledge God's love, God's treasures of mind, body and spirit may be revealed to you and become what you experience. This message has come to you at this time on your life's journey to assure you of God's love and power within you. You have called forth this knowing into your experience for you are connected with God's infinite source of wisdom. As you choose to proclaim and live the power of the words *"I love me,"* you can manifest God's treasures, resources and means for abundant, joyful and peaceful living.

Loving yourself acknowledges that you are Divinely connected to God's source of all love. During times when you are challenged to question the importance of loving yourself, simply return and dispel such false thinking to the light of God. Choosing to let *"I love me"* become your constant thought process and the words you vocalize even in the midst of what appears as chaos, brings forth God's power. It dispels those voices and negative thoughts that discourage you from accepting the love and power of God within you. The proclamation *"I love me"* solidifies your acceptance of God's essence and love within you where all power resides. You are the expression of God's loving essence. When you say *"I love me,"* you are accepting your oneness with the love and power of who God is. In your oneness with God, angels join with you to bear witness to God's light and love. It is this formidable love of God that reigns above all in creation. Through this profound awareness, you are taking part in the expression of God through you. As you do so, you become God's reflection of love in human form. In your choosing to say *"I love me,"* you can experience the joy of God's love and power that can bring forth harmony and peace in your relationships and in the world.

Statements To Voice For Victorious Living:

- I choose to say *"I love me."*
- I choose to be the expression of God's love.
- I choose God's infinite wisdom.
- I choose to be in oneness with the power of God's essence.
- I choose to walk in God's light.
- I choose to dispel all that is not of God's light.
- I choose the love and guidance of angels.
- I choose to accept the magnificence of who I am.
- I choose to be in exuberant joy.
- I choose be in gratitude.
- I choose to be thankful.
- I choose to be abundant.
- I choose to give and receive love.
- I choose peace and harmony.
- I choose to love and honor God.

As you so choose, so shall it be.

Honoring The Sacred Dwelling Place

The dwelling place is the sacred place within you where God's presence resides and from which God's love flows. When you choose to honor God's dwelling place by saying *"I love me,"* God's light and love empower you. It brings forth God's love and healing presence. As you walk your life's journey, angels join with you as your protectors and guides. Your time on this earth is given for you to know and experience the omnipresence of God. You are given unlimited opportunities to connect with and express God's presence and love. The magnificence of God instilled within the dwelling place is your source of abundant love. When you acknowledge God's love within you, you inhabit the dwelling place of God's love. Whatever place you are at during this time in your life, you have the authority of God to call forth His love and light to illuminate the path before you. We welcome you to this state of being, where the proclamation *"I love me"* brings forth the magnificence of God's dwelling place of love that is within you.

Welcome To The Celebration Of God's Love For You

Welcome to the celebration of God's love for you, where there is exuberant joy and the power of God's light. Life is meant for the celebration of God's unwavering love. It is meant for the celebration of God's creation of you. A celebration of love for God begins with the celebration of loving yourself. You are God's masterpiece created from His love with a bond that can never be broken. It is through this bond of love that the bountiful supply of God's riches in mind, body, and spirit is given. Angels join in the celebration of God's love for you. Awaken to the joy of who you are and go forth to share God's light and love with the world. In doing so, it will return to you in greater measure, and life will be the celebration of God's love as it was intended to be.

The angelic messages shared in this book have been given to assure you that you and God are Divinely connected. Proclaiming *"I love me"* and choosing to share God's love is a choice that can bring you to experience the immeasurable power of God's love and presence. As you say *"I love me"* and choose to receive and send forth God's love, you shall be a mighty force in the world.

The Light Of God Is Upon You

In your choosing to love yourself by saying *"I love me,"* the light of God is upon you. As you proceed on your life's journey, you have God's presence and authority to call forth God's love for healing and abundant living in your life and in the world. You inherit all that is of God's kingdom. You are being guided down the golden path before you by angels who come to give glory to God by loving you. Visualize your place in this peaceful and loving existence. See yourself creating life experiences that radiate God's joyous presence. All that has been revealed through the angelic message of *"I love me"* has come to bring an awakening within the souls of all people of the power of God's love and light. When you voice your love for God by saying *"I love me,"* your eyes will see, your heart will know, and your ears will hear what God has designed for you.

Through these messages you have been given full awareness and understanding that God's love is the source of all power. All other power is a fleeting illusion. Love does not ask you to harm, manipulate, control, or bring fear to another or to yourself. In God's light there is only love. All forms of hatred, violence, and control of one person over another are contrived forms of lower energy that must be dispelled to the light. God speaks to all people through a soul connection where God's essence abides. It is through your soul connection to God that Divine power and love are given and received. It is there that Divine wisdom is given to assist you in overcoming anything that attempts to distance you from God's love. When you say *"I love me,"* you become in oneness with your soul connection to God. As you love yourself and say

"I love me," you bring healing love into your life and into the world.

You are worthy of love and being loved, for God lives in you. At this time you are surrounded by God's love, and angels abide where you choose to go. In the path before you is this glorious view where the kingdom of God is filled with overflowing treasures for the love of you.

What Happens When You Are In A State Of *"I Love Me"*

When you say *"I love me,"* you are saying "I love God, who is within me." In this state of *"I love me,"* the love and power of God is made known to you. Those who come into your presence will experience the exuberant joy and love of God's presence. God's light will illuminate your path and will shine forth to bring light into the world. The signs of God's Divine grace and love will be seen throughout the universe. As you go forth, you will experience God's unwavering love for you.

In your expression of love for God, is the expression of your love for all of God's creation. Where there is love, there is light, and in the light there can be no darkness. You have God's light that overcomes the darkness. This is a time of rejoicing and exaltation, for the power that comes from saying *"I love me"* has now been revealed to you. You have the freedom and power to be who God created you to be. You have angels to enlighten you and guide your way. From this moment on, you can choose to be in oneness with God's love that is within you by saying *"I love me,"* and it shall be so.

CHAPTER ELEVEN

An Angel Message Of Reflection

My Dearest Children,

It is with exuberant joy that we come to converse with you. In the presence of God's love, we join with you and share in the glory of God's creation. You have been given the supreme awareness that God's love is within you. You have the power to create joyful and loving experiences, and to be a mighty force in the world. All that is given to you is created from God's perfection in spirit and love. God chose to call forth His light into you, for He has a design for your life. In the design of you is God's essence, which connects you to all that God is. In the design of you is God's perfection and all-knowing power. In the design of you is God's unwavering love assuring you of your place in the kingdom of God and all that is your inheritance. In the design of you is a knowing of God's blissful peace and wisdom, for the presence of God is within you.

You have been given a place in God's kingdom for you to receive all of His treasures. You are a part of the family of God. He designed you to know His exuberant love and to be empowered by His presence. You are connected to God's essence and you have the power of God's love to bring forth healing. We come to enlighten you to the presence of God's bountiful supply, which has no end. In your choosing to say *"I love me,"* you allow for the flow of God's bountiful supply in your life. Thoughts of a lack of power or a lack of love are thoughts to be eliminated and dispelled. God has no connection with such distortions of who you were created to be.

Our angelic messages are given to assure you of God's presence and love within you. They reveal that you are connected to God's source of love and power at all times. God has given you the gift of life to express His omnipresent power and love in the expression of who you are. Do not accept the false belief that you are not worthy of God's love or that God is sending pain and suffering to you. God loves you beyond measure. We know this to be truth that God instilled His love within you for you to be a reflection of His love and power. His love is within you for the expression of joyful and abundant living. We are with you to assist you in knowing the power of God's love and for you to experience all that God has designed for you.

When there appears to be any type of lack in body, mind, or spirit, call forth the power of God's love and light within you. God can do mighty things through you, for He created you in His image and instilled within you His power. There is no mountain that is insurmountable for God. There is no force that is greater than His love. God is the omnipresent powerful creator of the universe. He knows everything about you and watches every step that you take. He is present with you in this moment and His love is overflowing for you.

We have come to change any limited understanding you have of who you are and what you can become. You have the wisdom and formidable power of God within you. Within your soul are Divine truths of the magnitude of God's power and love. Spend time in adoration of God's presence within you by saying *"I love me."* This profound message is being brought to your awareness so that you can be the joyful expression of God's love. As you say *"I love me,"* you send forth God's love into your life and into the world. Accepting and sending forth God's love overcomes evil, plans for harm or destruction, and any form of lower energies such as fear, worry, anxiety and anger. When God's light and love are sent forth, the consciousness of the world vibrates at a higher Divine vibration of love. In this higher Divine vibration, love overcomes hatred and anger to bring harmony among people. When you say the words *"I love me,"* the power of God's love goes forth to affect the hearts and minds of people throughout the universe. As you rise up and claim your place in God's kingdom and voice *"I love me,"* you shall be in the company of angels to overcome fear and all negative forces or energies presented in the world.

In this moment, you can be the source of God's light and love to bring forth harmony and peace in the world. When you choose to love you, you empower yourself and others. There are legions of angels with forces beyond anything the world can contrive that can be called upon to assist you in overcoming anything not of God's light and love. The world depicted as dangerous and fearful has been created to inhibit your power. Do not accept it as so. Do not be manipulated by the illusion or the contrived way of thinking that there is much to fear in life. Let go of controlling negative thoughts that have no basis in God's creation. Accept that you are a being of God's light and allow the light to flow through you. Release the voices and thoughts in your mind that steal your energy, joy, peace, love, and power by returning them to God's light. Dispel any thoughts not of God's love or light and surrender them to God. When you are in a situation that presents fear, send forth God's light. Command the fear and all attachments to the fear to be dispelled into God's light. Do not resonate with or empower the fear in any manner. This will bring a peaceful state of mind, and quell the chatter in your thoughts that have no source in God's light. When you say *"I love me,"* God's abundant love flows from within you, and your life experiences become the expression of the infinitely loved being God created you to be. You shall witness the love of God to bring forth changes of great magnitude.

We come to assure you of our Divinely given role to walk your journey with you and to give glory to God in our assistance of you. We assure you that as you choose to send forth God's light and love into the world, God's powerful loving presence will be made known. It is in your acceptance of God's love and power within you that you can affect change within your life. We have shared the message of the power that comes from saying *"I love me,"* to bring all of creation into a harmonious existence with God. We are your devoted and loving angels, and we come to share in the exuberant joy of God's love with you. Call upon us, and we shall make our presence and the mighty power of God's love known to you. We assure you that you are loved beyond measure and we are always with you.

~Your Loving Angel Companions

CHAPTER TWELVE

Meet the Archangels

Archangels and their angel companions bring forth God's rays of light and are given powers to meet all of your needs. God has given angels the authority to share His Divine love and to perform specific services. The colors of the archangel rays signify the power given to them by God for the service that they provide for God's love and power to be manifested. They are bearers of God's light and bring forth love, truth, power and protection.

Angels make their presence known in many ways. They may flash their rays of colors through your thoughts, instill within you an inner calm, bring forth people and events to assist you, inspire you with words of wisdom, remove obstacles in your way, or reveal their presence in a vision. Angels are your Divine companions who honor God in their service of you. They have awareness of all the gifts God has created within you. They assist you in knowing the joy that comes from sharing and experiencing those gifts. Ask your archangels and angels for guidance, direction and protection on the path that you walk and they will joyfully intervene for you. Whatever the means an angel chooses to make God's love and power known to you, be assured they are with you in every moment and have God's authority to minister to you.

The Seven Archangels And The Services They Provide		
Archangel	Color of Ray	Services For
Michael	Blue	Divine Power; Protection From Terror Aggression, Evil, Accidents, Crime; Spiritual, Mental and Physical Harm; Provides Strength, Courage, Integrity
Jophiel	Yellow	Divine Wisdom, Truth, Illumination, Clarity, Insight, Loving Thoughts, Self-esteem, Self-confidence; Help with Studying, Exams and Tests; Addictions
Chamuel	Pink	Divine Love and Compassion; Comfort; Companionship; Relationship Healing; Peaceful and Loving Relationships; Finding a Job; Locating a Lost Object

Gabriel	White	Divine Enlightenment; Revelation; Purity; Peace of Mind; Life, Career, and Educational Decisions; Inspiration; Assistance with Money and Resources
Raphael	Green	Divine Healing in Mind, Body and Spirit; Addictions and Cravings; Safe Travel; Help with Food; Clothing and Shelter; Exposing Truth and Lies
Uriel	Gold	Divine Peace, Harmony, Intellectual Understanding, Resolution to Problems, Ending of Wars, Help with The Weather And Natural Disasters, Release of Fear

Zadkiel	Violet	Divine Freedom, Mercy, Inner Peace, Forgiveness, Renewal of Spirit, Release of Past Traumas, Painful Memories, Negative Traits and Feelings, For Joy

Archangel Michael

Archangel Michael ministers the power of God's love through the blue with gold and white rays of light for Divine protection and power.

Call upon Archangel Michael to send forth God's light and love for spiritual and physical protection, courage, strength, power, truth and integrity. Archangel Michael brings forth God's Divine forces to dispel evil and overcome fear, anger, worry, anxiety, and despair. Ask Archangel Michael for protection from crimes, accidents, terror, aggression, psychic attacks, or any attempts to harm you. Archangel Michael has the power to eliminate the forces of darkness and evil. He helps you to be courageous and strong. Archangel Michael encourages your worthiness and self-esteem by removing your doubts.

Prayer to Archangel Michael

Archangel Michael, I ask you to be my companion and to send forth upon me God's Divine light for protection of my mind, body and spirit. Archangel Michael, I call upon you to protect me from any physical, mental, or spiritual attacks, terror, aggression, evil and harm. Archangel Michael, inspire, strengthen, and guide me to be in oneness with God's love and power. Archangel Michael, surround me with your light and send forth your power to dispel the forces of darkness and evil, and to remove my fears, anxieties, doubts and worries. Thank you Archangel Michael for sending forth God's Divine light, love, power, protection, and healing upon me and upon this world.

I Love Me. And so it is."

Archangel Jophiel

Archangel Jophiel ministers the power of God's love through the yellow with gold rays of light for Divine wisdom, truth, intuition, clarity, insight, and loving thoughts.

Call upon Archangel Jophiel to send forth God's light and love for Divine wisdom, truth, insight, intuition, inspiration, clarity, joy, laughter and illumination of loving and beautiful thoughts. Archangel Jophiel brings God's wisdom, joy and laughter to help free you from anything that blocks your oneness with God. Archangel Jophiel sends forth inspiration and clarity to help you see God's goodness and beauty in life. Archangel Jophiel removes negative thoughts and inspires self-love, self-esteem, and self-confidence. Archangel Jophiel can be called upon for help with overcoming addictions. Ask Archangel Jophiel for assistance with your studies, when taking tests and exams, concentrating, focusing, and making presentations.

Prayer to Archangel Jophiel

Archangel Jophiel, I ask you to be my companion and to send forth upon me God's Divine light for wisdom, intuition, insight, truth, inspiration, clarity, and joyful thoughts. Archangel Jophiel, inspire, strengthen and guide me to be in oneness with God's love and power. Archangel Jophiel, surround me with your light and send forth your power to dispel the forces of darkness and evil, and to remove my fears, worries, anxieties, negative thoughts and addictions. Archangel Jophiel, I ask you to send forth God's light of wisdom for success in my studies and when taking tests. Archangel Jophiel, inspire me to see the goodness, beauty and joy in life. Thank you Archangel Jophiel for sending forth God's Divine light, love, power, wisdom and healing upon me and upon this world. *I Love Me*. And so it is."

Archangel Chamuel

Archangel Chamuel ministers the power of God's love through the pink with rose rays of light for Divine unconditional love and compassion.

Call upon Archangel Chamuel to send forth God's unconditional Divine love and compassion to help you to honor and love yourself and others. Archangel Chamuel assists with creating loving, peaceful, personal and professional relationships, finding companionship, and resolving relationship conflicts and problems. Archangel Chamuel intercedes to bring love and harmony when there is conflict between a parent and a child. Archangel Chamuel will bring forth love, assistance and comfort when there is a divorce, separation, or death of a loved one. Call upon Archangel Champed to help with finding a job and locating something that is lost.

Prayer to Archangel Chamuel

Archangel Chamuel, I ask you to be my companion and to send forth upon me God's Divine light for unconditional love to fill my heart with love for myself and for others. Archangel Chamuel, I ask you to comfort and uplift me, and to help me form loving companionship. Archangel Chamuel, I call upon you to help me to resolve any personal or professional relationship conflicts, troubles or problems. Archangel Chamuel, I ask for your assistance to help me to find employment that will bring abundance and enjoyment into my life. Archangel Chamuel, inspire, strengthen and guide me to be in oneness with God's love and power. Archangel Chamuel, send forth your power to dispel the forces of darkness and evil. Archangel Chamuel, I ask you to bring harmony, understanding, peace and love within my relationships, family, community and within the world. Thank you Archangel Chamuel for sending forth God's Divine light, love, power and healing upon me and upon this world. *I Love Me.* And so it is.

Archangel Gabriel

Archangel Gabriel ministers the power of God's love through the white with gold rays of light for Divine enlightenment, prophecy, revelation, purity and peace of mind.

Call upon Archangel Gabriel to send forth God's light and love for enlightenment, prophecy, revelation, guidance and peace of mind. Archangel Gabriel is God's messenger who brings Divine guidance and helps you to choose which direction and path to take. Ask Archangel Gabriel to intercede if you are trying to have a child. Archangel Gabriel inspires and assists with career, educational, and life decisions. Archangel Gabriel helps with finding a job, and attaining money and resources to bring harmony and balance into your life. Ask Archangel Gabriel to remove discouragement, despair, doubt, fear, worry, and negative influences. Archangel Gabriel brings inspiration and intuition to walk in God's light for victorious living.

Prayer to Archangel Gabriel

Archangel Gabriel, I ask you to be my companion and to send forth upon me God's Divine light for enlightenment, inspiration, peace of mind, prophecy and revelation. Archangel Gabriel, inspire, strengthen and guide me to be in oneness with God's love and power. Archangel Gabriel, inspire and assist me in making life, career and educational decisions that will lead me on a path to victorious and joyful living. Archangel Gabriel, I ask for your assistance to help me to find employment that will bring abundance and enjoyment into my life. Archangel Gabriel, I ask you to send forth your power to dispel the forces of darkness and evil and to remove from me any discouragement, despair, doubt, worry, anxiety, depression, fear, and negative influences. Thank you Archangel Gabriel for sending forth God's Divine light, love, power and healing upon me and upon this world. *I Love Me.* And so it is.

Archangel Raphael

Archangel Raphael ministers the power of God's love through the green with white and gold rays of light for Divine healing.

Call upon Archangel Raphael to send forth God's light and love for healing in mind, body, and spirit. Archangel Raphael assists with all forms of healing, inspires new cures for diseases, and helps to eliminate addictions and cravings. Call upon Archangel Raphael when you have any type of illness and need healing. Archangel Raphael discerns truth, exposing untruth and dishonesty. Ask Archangel Raphael to assist you with safe travel and with your needs for food, clothing and shelter.

Prayer to Archangel Raphael

Archangel Raphael, I ask you to be my companion and to send forth upon me God's Divine light for healing of my body, mind and spirit. Archangel Raphael, I call upon your power and intervention to supply my needs for food, clothing and shelter, and to keep me safe in my travels. Archangel Raphael, inspire, strengthen and guide me to be in oneness with God's love and power. Archangel Raphael, I ask you to inspire new cures for diseases, and to eliminate addictions and cravings. Archangel Raphael, send forth your power to dispel the forces of darkness and evil and to discern the truth, exposing untruth and dishonesty. Thank you Archangel Raphael for sending forth God's Divine light, love, power and healing upon me and upon this world. *I Love Me*. And so it is.

Archangel Uriel

Archangel Uriel ministers the power of God's love through the gold with purple, white, and rose rays of light for Divine peace and harmony.

Call upon Archangel Uriel to send forth God's light and love for peace, tranquility, harmony, understanding, forgiveness, insight and intellectual information. Archangel Uriel brings inspiration and helps in resolving conflicts for harmonious personal and professional relationships. Archangel Uriel brings Divine justice in the courtroom and among nations, and assists with problem solving by providing answers and practical solutions. Archangel Uriel helps release anger, fear, worry, and anxiety for peace of mind and healing. Call upon Archangel Uriel to bring peace, harmony and brotherhood in the world, and to end wars and fighting. Archangel Uriel helps with the weather and brings protection from manmade or natural disasters such as fires, earthquakes, hurricanes, tornadoes and floods to keep you safe and to recover in the aftermath. Archangel Uriel helps bring the universal consciousness in the world to one of peace and love.

Prayer to Archangel Uriel

Archangel Uriel, I ask you to be my companion and to send forth God's Divine light upon me for peace,

Angels Share the Power of "I Love Me"

tranquility, harmony, understanding, forgiveness, and insight. Archangel Uriel, surround me with your light and send forth your power to dispel the forces of darkness and evil and to bring an end to fighting, discord, terror and war. Archangel Uriel, help there to be peace, understanding and harmony between all people. Archangel Uriel, I ask you to protect me from manmade and natural disasters, and destructive changes in the weather. Archangel Uriel, inspire, strengthen and guide me to be in oneness with God's love and power. Thank you Archangel Uriel for sending forth God's Divine light, love, peace, power and healing upon me and upon this world. *I Love Me*. And so it is.

127

Archangel Zadkiel

Archangel Zadkiel ministers the power of God's love through the violet and purple with white rays of light for Divine freedom, mercy, inner peace, joy, forgiveness, and the renewal of spirit.

Call upon Archangel Zadkiel to send forth God's light and love to dissolve painful memories, past traumas, judgments, emotional issues, negative thoughts and feelings. Archangel Zadkiel helps you to have mercy, compassion, justice, and forgiveness toward yourself and others. Archangel Zadkiel clears your heart of pain and suffering. Archangel Zadkiel inspires peaceful agreements and justice between warring people. Archangel Zadkiel brings soul freedom, inner power, and joy.

Prayer to Archangel Zadkiel

Archangel Zadkiel, I ask you to be my companion and to send forth upon me God's Divine light for inner peace, joy, forgiveness and freedom from painful memories, past traumas, judgments, emotional issues, negative thoughts, feelings and actions. Archangel Zadkiel, I ask you to inspire, strengthen and guide me to be in oneness with God's love and power. Archangel Zadkiel, surround me with your light and send forth your power to dispel the forces of darkness and evil.

Archangel Zadkiel, I call upon you to help me to know inner peace, joy, mercy and compassion, and to have forgiveness toward myself and others. Thank you Archangel Zadkiel for sending forth God's Divine love, power, joy, forgiveness and healing upon me and upon this world. *I Love Me.* And so it is.

Angels Are Your Loving Companions

Angels are your loving companions who are always with you. When you ask angels to assist you, they joyfully do so. They come to shine God's light upon you for you to know the joy and power of God's unconditional love in your life. They have God's authority to minister to your needs and to bring healing to your mind, body and spirit. They bring to your awareness what God has designed for your well-being and guide you on the path that you walk. They help you to see the beauty and joy in life. The angelic messages in this book are being shared so that you can know God's unwavering love for you, and the power of the words *"I love me"* to bring forth love, joy, beauty, healing and power in your life.

You are the bearer of God's love and it is your choice how you express the love of God. In each moment you have the opportunity to choose and to send forth God's love and light. In each moment you have the connection to God's power that brings forth healing of mind, body, and spirit.

When you say *"I love me,"* you surround yourself and receive the power of God's light. As God's light flows through you, it expands out into the universe to create experiences of joy, love and healing. When you choose to say *"I love me,"* you enrich your life with God's grace and love. In doing so, you enrich and change the world for the glory of God and His loving presence to be made known.

Your Acceptance For The Assistance of Angels And What God Has Designed For You

I give thanks to my angel companions for their love, guidance and assistance in helping me to become all that God has created me to be. I am in gratitude for the awareness that all that is within me is in likeness to God, who created me from His love. I know that as I love myself and say *"I love me,"* I love God who is within me. I accept that within my soul and heart consciousness I have a loving connection to God and His power. I accept that I am in oneness with the love and power of God within me. I accept with gratitude God's love and the Divine inheritance that is mine as His child. I accept all the treasures that God has created within His kingdom for me. I accept God's wisdom to guide and inspire me. I accept God's abundant health and well-being in my mind, body and spirit. I accept God's forgiveness and I choose to forgive others. I accept God's creation of loving, peaceful and harmonious relationships. I accept God's abundance and prosperity in all manners and ways. I accept with gratitude the companionship of angels who shine God's light and love upon me. I accept God's presence, love, light and power within me. I shall honor God by proclaiming now and into eternity *"I Love Me."* And so it is.

HIGHLIGHTS OF ANGELIC MESSAGES

- When you say *"I love me,"* you are saying "I love God who is within me."
- In choosing to say *"I love me,"* you are honoring God and giving glory for God's presence that is within you.
- God is love, and His love is always and forever within you.
- *"I love me"* can overcome any bondage or negative energy that blocks your connection to God.
- When you say *"I love me,"* there is no space within you for self-judgment, self-criticism, or self-hatred.
- In your choosing to love yourself, you are making it known to the universe that you are worthy of love.
- Loving yourself acknowledges that you are Divinely connected to God's source of all love.
- The more you say *"I love me"* and acknowledge God's love, the more love will inhabit your being and become your experience.
- Each time you say *"I love me,"* it has immediate effects upon your life and within the world.
- God created you, and your life is of extreme importance.

- You walk your path in the company of angels and they are always with you.
- In choosing to say *"I love me,"* you immediately call forth the love and power of God that is within you.
- Angels are sent by God to enlighten and assist you to experience the magnificence of who God is within you.
- Joining with others who resonate self-love will bring the consciousness of your world to a loving state of being.
- The understanding of the words *"I love me"* has been shared for their power to bring changes of Divine magnitude.
- *"I love me"* in its very expression enlists the power and guidance of angels for the glorious expression of you.
- *"I love me"* brings forth a joyous state of being.
- You abide in God's presence.
- As you choose to say *"I love me,"* you choose to be a vessel for the power of God's love to flow throughout the universe.
- The words *"I love me"* have been Divinely given to assure you of the power of God's love and to show you how to be victorious in your life.
- When you accept that you are connected to God's essence, you accept God's power within

you to resonate love even to those you have never met.

- You have God's power in this moment to dispel anything not of God's love and light.
- The joy of who you are as Divinely created by God is what has been given to you as your inheritance.
- As you say *"I love me,"* you shall witness the magnitude of God's love in all forms.
- You do not walk your journey in life alone. You always have God's ministering angels with you.
- When you say *"I love me,"* you empower the creation and coming together of all that is in the universe, to bring joy and love into your existence.
- By loving yourself, you love God who is within you.
- It is love that awakens the truth within you of the abundant power you have to be all that is of God.
- Life is meant for the celebration and glorious expression of God's love.
- You can choose to accept God's love and power within you, and it shall be so.
- You can choose to call forth the love and guidance of angels, and it shall be so.
- Your life is not measured in days but in expressions of who you choose to be.

- You are a vessel of God's love and light that beams stronger and brighter when you choose to say *"I love me."*
- Angels can intercede for you to bring all things into existence for the expression of God's love.
- There are no forces that have greater power in your life than God.
- When you choose to say *"I love me,"* you shall overcome the thoughts and views that create fear.
- Choosing to say *"I love me"* is your spiritual warfare to dispel and overcome fear and anything that is not of God's light.
- God has designed you to be an expression of His love and power.
- Each person has been given free will to choose to accept and to share God's love.
- When you choose to love yourself and say *"I love me,"* you give honor to God.
- We come to share this truth that the love that is within you connects you to God and to all creation.
- When you express *"I love me,"* there is no judgment of you or others.
- Self-love is a form of love that aligns you with the love of God. It brings the joy of God's presence and healing power into your world.

- When you say *"I love me,"* you are acknowledging God created you and His presence is instilled within you.
- Self-love connects you to God's love, and is a powerful means by which you create peace, harmony, and joy in your life, and in the world.
- Angels are your companions, and when you rejoice, they rejoice with you.
- Angels send messages through the people and events that cross your path to assure you that you are being guided in God's light.
- All knowledge is within you for which path to take and angels shall bring this knowledge to your awareness.
- God's love has been brought forth in human form for God chose to dwell within you.
- Angels take joy in walking your journey with you.
- You have within you a storehouse of wisdom and information beyond all that you know.
- As you honor and love yourself, your experiences change to align with the worthiness of who you are as a child of God.
- Choosing to love yourself and saying *"I love me"* allows God's love to go forth, creating experiences that reflect the joy and love within you.

- In God's decrees, all are formed in the image of God, and all have God's authority to send forth His light and love for healing in the world.
- It is not by might that you overcome the lower energies and the forces of untruth, but by the power of God's love within you.
- You can banish anything not of God's light by choosing to dispel it back to God's light.
- God's essence of love is within you and within all of creation, and it has power over all that exists.
- To be truly abundant is to know God's love for you and to share God's love with others.
- In every moment you can choose to say *"I love me,"* and the Divine expression of your magnificence shall manifest.
- Life is a presentation of the magnitude of God's endless blessings and opportunities to express His Divinity within you.
- The proclamation *"I love me"* is your acceptance of all the love, joy, treasures and blessings God had designed for you.
- God honors your choices to love yourself and that creates new and loving experiences.
- Loving yourself is a choice that brings forth your Divine inheritance.

- When you say *"I love me,"* you accept the love of God within you that holds all His treasures for you.
- You are being awakened to the power of God's essence and love that inhabits who you are.
- You send God's love into the world each time you say *"I love me."*
- When you say *"I love me,"* you love and honor God.
- In each moment there is a seed within you of God's infinite love and Divine possibilities to be all that you are created to be.
- There is a Divine spiritual vibration within these three words, *"I love me."* The mere thought of these words can raise your consciousness for experiencing God's love.
- When you say *"I love me,"* you send out a powerful vibration of love that has an effect upon the consciousness of the world.
- The love that you send forth can touch the soul of another to create a peaceful and loving existence.
- When you say *"I love me,"* you shall experience many signs of God's love in your life.
- In your choosing to say *"I love me,"* you experience the joy of God's essence and healing power that shall bring forth harmony in the world.

- Your time on this earth is given for you to know and experience the omnipresence of God.
- The dwelling place is the sacred place within you where God's presence resides and from which God's love flows.
- We welcome you to this state of being, where the proclamation *"I love me"* brings forth the magnificence of who God is within you.
- You are God's masterpiece that was created from love with His bond that can never be broken.
- You are being guided down the golden path before you by angels who come to give glory to God by loving you.
- As you proceed on your life's journey, you have God's presence and authority to call forth God's love for healing and abundant living in your life and in the world.
- When you voice your proclamation of your love for God by saying *"I love me,"* your eyes will see, your heart will know, and your ears will hear what God has designed for you.
- You are worthy of love and being loved, for God lives in you.
- When you say *"I love me,"* you are saying, "I love God who is within me."
- When you say *"I love me,"* you become in oneness with your soul connection to God.

141

- Angels welcome you to the celebration of God's love for you, where there is exuberant joy and the overflowing power of God's light.
- In each moment there is the seed of life waiting to burst forth with God's inheritance for you.
- Life is meant for the celebration of God's unwavering love and God's creation of you.

Go Forth In The
Power of God's
Light and Love
And Proclaim
The Words

"I Love Me"